Published by the Wymondham Heritage Society
10 The Bridewell, Norwich Road, Wymondham NR18 0NS
Registered charity No. 299548

ISBN 1 - 901553 - 07 - 8

First published in 2004

The Wymondham Heritage Society
publishes a number of booklets about Wymondham,
obtainable from Wymondham Heritage Museum

INTRODUCTION

HOW 'THE WYMONDHAM STORY' BEGAN IN 2000

'The Wymondham Story' was originally conceived as a plan to celebrate the Millennium during Museums & Galleries Week in 2000, by promoting community awareness of local history and heritage. The project, which received an Awards for All Lottery grant, was a guided walk around Wymondham, covering 1000 years of its history. During the walk a narrator introduced various costumed historical characters, who explained their roles at important stages in Wymondham's history.

In this booklet I have adapted and revised the information used in the walk and some new material has been added. In the walk the characters, based on real historical figures, were played by a wide cross-section of the local community. They reappear here together with the additional ones I have researched to 'fill out' the story. The role of the narrator has been expanded to link the characters more fully to their historical background.

I have tried to portray in outline a 1000 years of Wymondham's history, by focusing briefly on different types of people and important episodes in the story – hence 'snapshot' in the title of this booklet. Some of the characters included were important and influential, others were ordinary but happened to live at interesting points in the Wymondham story.

This booklet is about the people, places and events which are part of Wymondham's history. Inevitably much has been omitted in this personal portrait, but I have tried to convey the substance of the story and something of the character of this historic Norfolk town.

I hope also that some sense of where Wymondham fits into the national story will be appreciated. Wymondham has many facets and is a product of a long and complex evolution over many centuries. This is an attempt to re-create that story in an unusual manner by providing a permanent record of an event which brought the history and heritage of Wymondham to life in an open and accessible way.

ACKNOWLEDGMENTS

I am very grateful to the following people who dressed up in period costume, learned their lines and entertained the walkers in the 'Wymondham Story' in 2000; also those who took part in the offshoot event, the 'Bridewell Story' in 2002. They were enthusiastic, supportive and very convincing.

Graham Barrell, Bob McClenning, Rev Brian Gant, Russell Turner, Kevin Oelrichs, David Chisnell, Alice Chisnell, Helen Cubitt, John Wilson, Bert Eke, Mike and Billy Smith, Martin Spriggs, the late Graham Knight, Eric Thorburn, Jeff Byron, Peter James, Stuart Webber, Jenny James, Barbara Tilly, Claire Furness, Ruth and Ann Charles, Janet Smith, Georgette Vale, Barry Kendrick, Horace Wilkinson, David Turner, Chris Fiddiman, Ron Hyam, Penny Barrell, Neil Storey, Sarah Storey, Mr and Mrs Keith Thomas, Amanda Oelrichs.

Their photographs were taken by Terry Burchell and I am extremely grateful to Terry for allowing me to copy and use them here.

The photographs of George Edwards and Edwin Gooch and Harold Crane were kindly loaned by Philip Yaxley. Mrs Molly Welfare (née Stone), a former evacuee in Wymondham, kindly lent the photographs of her time in the town during the war years. Incidentally, Molly's memories, together with those of other evacuees are the basis of the character Molly, an evacuee, in this booklet. Anne Edwards and Mary Childerhouse have kindly let me use photographs about the Briton Brush factory and I am also grateful to Michael Marwood for his contribution to the brushmaking section. The photograph of a scene from the re-enactment of Kett's Rebellion in 1999, is by kind permission of Stewart Goodman. Janet Smith and Mary Garner, those stalwarts of the Town Archive, have provided me with excellent service and support while researching material for this project, which has been much appreciated. Rosemary Charles, John Wilson, Philip Yaxley, Mary Garner, Jenny Pavey, Brenda Garrard and Brenda Ford kindly read the typescript, pointed out errors and made other useful suggestions. The imperfections which remain are entirely my responsibility.

Finally, I am as ever, indebted to my wife Anne. She has made a huge contribution to the production of this work including line drawings, maps, the general lay-out and much, much more. Her enthusiasm for this project has made it enjoyable and, I hope, worthwhile.

PART ONE

THE MEDIEVAL CENTURIES 1000 - 1500

THE NORMAN IMPACT - PRIORY, CHURCH AND CHAPEL 1066 - 1200

The story begins with Wymondham Abbey whose founder William d'Albini, was from one of the most important families in England after the Norman Conquest. He was given the manor of Wymondham as a reward for his family's services in 1066. Forty years later he was planning the foundation of a monastery there for a prior, 12 monks and a church, It was endowed by the grant of large estates, including part of his manor of Wymondham and built on the site of an earlier Saxon church.

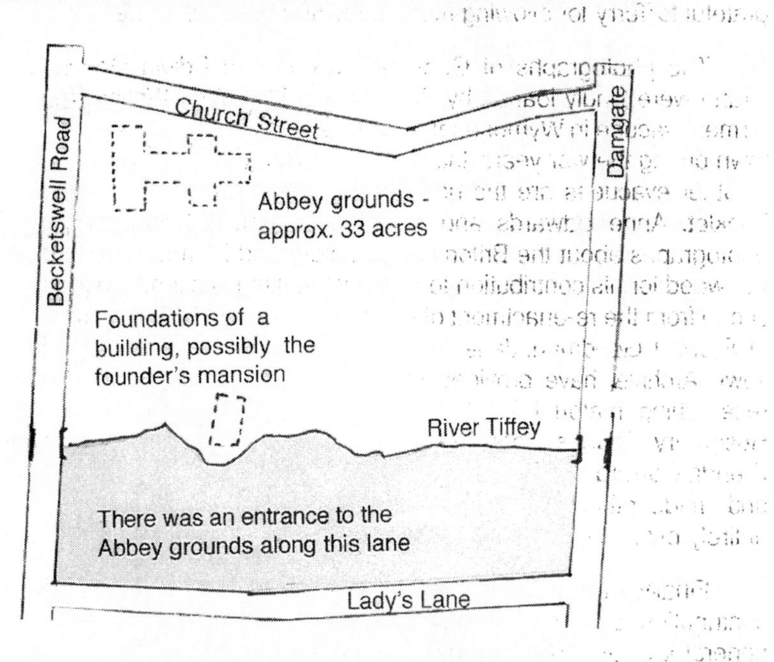

The Abbey site in the early 12th century, with modern street pattern

Building begins

Work on Wymondham Priory began in 1107. Stone was brought from Caen in northern France, the last stages of its journey along the river Tiffey. The old Saxon church on the site was pulled down and the new Norman building began.

William d'Albini also founded Westwode Chapel for lepers just outside the town.

Thomas Martin's impression of Westwode Chapel

Some years later in 1174, d'Albini's son, also William, built Becket's Chapel in honour of the murdered archbishop Thomas a Becket. Becket became a popular saint in the town which was a magnet for medieval pilgrims.

By 1130 the church, dedicated to St Mary and St Alban, was complete and extensive monastic buildings on the south side facing the Tiffey were appearing. The Normans were transforming the oldest religious site in Wymondham.

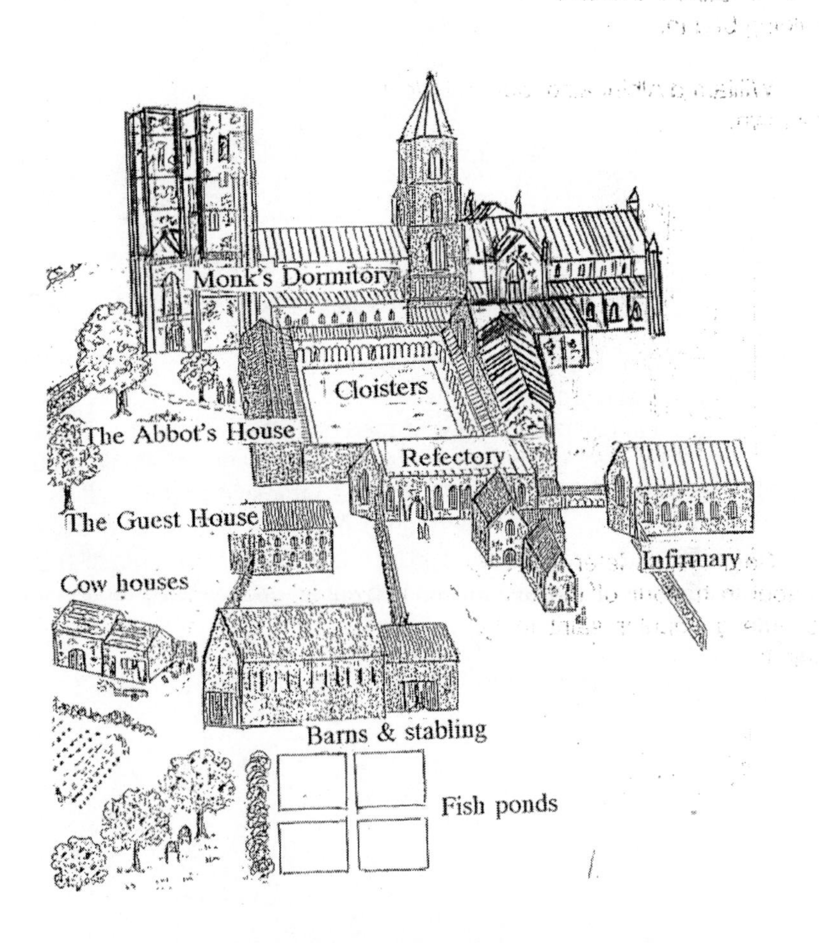

Artist's impression of the later phase of the monastic buildings 1175 - 1400

A 19TH CENTURY DISCOVERY

The abbey remains in the 1830s

On a cold December day in 1834, Samuel Woodward, a noted antiquarian, was in Wymondham for an excavation to witness the opening of two leaden coffins discovered by workmen near the high altar in the abbey ruins. Woodward, John Dalrymple, a surgeon, and a small group of interested observers hovered with intense curiosity as the coffins were opened. In the larger one an excellently preserved mummified body was revealed, still with a mass of curling auburn hair. The smaller coffin poignantly revealed a tiny mummified body of an unborn baby removed from its mother.

Plan showing position of the two coffins found in 1833

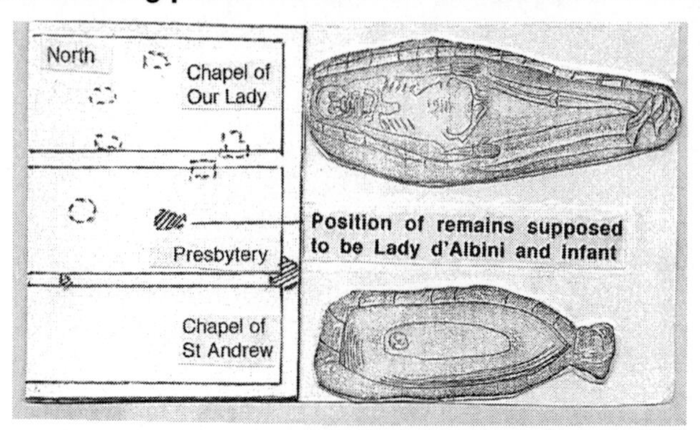

Samuel Woodward, an antiquarian

We concluded that because the bodies were buried near the high altar, they were of a young mother of high rank who had died before giving birth to her baby.

Locals had talked of seeing a golden cradle among the monastic ruins. Doubtless the story of the infant's burial has been handed down by many generations and become 'gilded' in the minds of the people.

Had the larger coffin not been fractured some years before, when the vault was accidentally opened, I am convinced that the body of the mother would almost certainly have equalled in quality of preservation the best examples of the Egyptians. In this coffin we found cumin and coriander seeds which gave off a pleasant perfume.

The two bodies in the coffins were those of Maude, the young wife of William d'Albini, founder of Wymondham Priory, and their unborn daughter.

The troubles between Priory and Church

These began when Nigel was appointed first prior at Wymondham in 1130, because he nominated secular clergy for the parish church according to the wishes of the founder. The prior claimed jurisdiction over the whole building which annoyed the parishioners who believed they were responsible for the parish church. In 1221 Walter was appointed by the prior as the first vicar proper, but it was not long before his independence was being challenged by the prior.

The situation was aggravated by the failure of the founder to indicate which part of the church he had built was for the monastery and which for the parish. This vagueness was a recipe for problems causing friction between the monks and parishioners who shared the same building. These disputes lasted for over 300 years. Feelings ran high and in 1249 the Pope decreed that the church did have a separate status under the supervision of its vicar. The Pope also designated which part of the buildings was for the parish and which for the monastery. Unfortunately there was no actual partition in the building so difficulties continued.

Another complication was the interference by the Abbot of St Albans who claimed the right to appoint the prior, though the founder's charter had stated the prior should be elected by the monks and then confirmed by the patron. So alongside the disputes between monks and parishioners there was also conflict between descendants of the d'Albinis and the Abbots of St Albans. Furthermore, the Bishop of Norwich also claimed some authority over the monastery which was within his diocese. The situation was fraught with problems.

On the one hand, the monks or regulars were bound by the rules of the Benedictine Order and subject to the authority of the prior. On the other, the parish clergy or seculars and the parishioners were under the control of the Archdeacon and Bishop of Norwich. Differences and conflict between the two were inevitable. This rivalry was further exacerbated when the seculars, usually nominated by the lord of the manor, were in the case of Wymondham appointed by the prior as decreed by William d'Albini.

The Abbot and Vicar discuss their differences

Father William Bokenham, Abbot of Wymondham, 1466-71

I am the second abbot of this Benedictine monastery which has been an independent abbey since 1448, and the first to be elected by my brother monks. But for nearly 350 years since 1107 when William d'Albini founded the priory here, our community was ruled by the Abbot of St Albans.

During those centuries, the priors oversaw to the best of their ability, the services in the church which we share with the town's parishioners, the first I believe, to be built for joint use by monks and townspeople. Unfortunately as we know there have been disputes and bad feeling between the monastery and town, marred on many occasions by unseemly violence.

It is good that the abbey church has been re-dedicated to St Mary and St Thomas in honour of the saintly Becket, whose chapel is nearby.

Thomas Draper Vicar of Wymondham, 1466-79

But the parishioners were naturally angered by the prior's claim to jurisdiction over the whole building which prevented the parish clergy from having any control over the town's church. Remember that the Pope himself investigated the situation here in 1249 and decreed that the church and monastery were to be separate. He also set out which parts of the building belonged to each, granting us the nave and north aisle.

Earlier this century, the monks again annoyed the townsfolk when they rebuilt their east tower (the octagon) further west and made matters worse by constructing a wall across the nave which obstructed the parish congregation's view of the high altar. We all worship the same God, Father William, and such conduct naturally upset the parishioners.

Abbot

But did that justify the parishioners ringing bells while the monks were at divine service, locking the prior in a tower, stopping the monks collecting their share of the offerings and breaking into the prior's lodge? Such conduct, for which they were ordered to keep the peace, is most unfitting for those who profess to worship God and live in peace.

Vicar

Of course I too condemn such behaviour, but it was surely equally unfitting for the monks to set squints in their dormitory wall above the south aisle to spy on the parishioners in their church. I can understand why feeling ran so high. Remember that King Henry VI ordered the Archbishop of Canterbury to investigate the problems in 1412 and he re-affirmed the Papal decision of 1249 which restored our rights.

Abbot

Yes, but even then the town wasn't satisfied and began to campaign for a massive new west tower which almost dwarfs our beautiful octagon tower.

Vicar

We are proud of this tower. It is a symbol of the church's power and independence. Besides, you removed our bells to the monastery and we need our own tower in which the church bells can be hung to summon the parishioners to worship. We are grateful to Sir John Clifford and others who supported the campaign to build this tower.

Abbot

Although relations between us have been bitter and unseemly for so long, I think we both recognise it is time to put our differences behind us and live together peacefully in this beautiful building, serving God and the community. As you know we cultivate our lands, breed fish, allow local farmers to graze our meadows, befriend the poor and sick and welcome travellers and pilgrims who come to this special place. Also of course we educate those townspeople who wish to learn.

Vicar

I agree. Just as you are pleased to be independent of St Albans, so the parishioners are pleased to manage their own church with a tower which symbolises our independence of the monastery. But I am sure we can remain good neighbours living in peace and harmony together.

Abbot

It is good to be part of a new era of peace and goodwill between our two communities. God grant our modus vivendi will long continue.

The lengthy conflict between monks and parishioners finally came to an end in the 15th century. It was at the core of the history of medieval Wymondham.

THE PEASANTS REVOLT 1381

In 1381 the 'poore commons' rose in revolt against the hated Poll Tax introduced by Richard II to pay for the disastrous war against France. Wat Tyler the peasant leader marched on London from Kent, while in Norfolk Geoffrey Litster of Felmingham, 'king of the commons', assembled with his followers on Mousehold Heath. They entered Norwich and raided properties of hated officials. Elsewhere in Norfolk they targeted oppressive landowners, hoping to destroy their court and manorial records which gave them their power over the peasantry. In Wymondham the local peasantry found their own leader.

John Bettes, local leader during the Peasants Revolt

We poor peasants are borne down by heavy taxes but the Poll Tax is one too many for the likes of me, a poor tanner by trade. We are under the yoke of the landlords and do their bidding by working on their estates; we are little more than slaves and are punished if we dare ask for a better wage for honest labour. Some 30 year ago (1349) during the plague - Black Death we called it - a third or so of the people round here died. After that we had hoped our labour be better rewarded. But still we're crushed by powerful, corrupt men.

So I decided to follow Litster's example. I raised a 'society', that is a group of like-minded men from around Wymondham like John Spicer. We stole gold coins and goods from John de Harley, a JP at Harling. Then we attacked the properties of rich officials including the hated poll tax collector John Reed of Rougham. He's abused his powers as landowner and manorial lord. Then we assembled with two other bands and ripped up and burned charters, deeds and court records belonging to John de Palgrave. We destroyed anything which landowners used to oppress us. We're not murderers or looters, but simply poor men seeking justice.

Eventually I was arrested but they could prove nothing against me and I was later released. But the brave Litster and his men were defeated near North Walsham and he was executed by the Bishop of Norwich.

Now the great revolt is over. Litster and Tyler are dead but our struggle to raise the poor peasantry from near slavery to a better position will go on. We lit a candle this summer and God willing, it will not be put out.

PART TWO

THE TUDOR CENTURY 1485-1603

Peace between Abbey and Church c 1470- 1520

After 350 years of strife, relations between monks and parishioners entered a more settled and peaceful phase. Townspeople came to hold the abbey in affection. Some were tenants, the poor grazed their livestock on the abbey meadows, some served as churchwardens and servers in the abbey church. Wymondham enjoyed a period of growing prosperity and the religious renown associated with the abbey and its church, Becket's Chapel and Becket's Well ensured a steady flow of visitors to the town.

The decline of Wymondham Abbey

However, all was not well behind the abbey walls. Signs of a fall from the high standards of the Benedictines were revealed during the visitation to the abbey by the Bishop of Norwich in 1492. His report shows that laxity had crept in and that the monks were finding the Benedictine rules irksome - they went hunting, and mixed freely with the townspeople buying and selling goods in the town like merchants.They were not in the cloisters for the required times and were neglecting repairs to the buildings. The temptations of the secular world were proving irresistible.

All this would make the task of Henry VIII's officials easier, when they came to dissolve the monastery in the 1530s.

The Bishop's visit to Wymondham Abbey in 1514

During another visitation, the Bishop of Norwich Richard Nix, spoke to many of the monks and discovered a further disturbing decline in their behaviour. One of the monks he met was Thomas Lynn.

Bishop Richard

The prior tells me that women suspiciously frequent the passage to the chamber of brother James Blome the Chamberlain, including the daughters of a certain widow residing in Le Dairie who also come suspiciously to his chamber. I am also informed that the brothers are unwilling to study and do not attend matins, that the ornaments of the church suffer great decay and the Chamberlain does not provide light for the dormitory or presbytery. Two brothers wear shirts and long boots, another is drunk while another uses opprobrious language. Most disturbing is that none of the monks provide for the children in the almonry school run for the children of the town as a charity.

Brother Thomas Lynn

It is true that the brothers are unwilling to come to matins and hardly to compline. Indeed scarcely 3-4 monks are present at matins. I know too that brother Richard Cambridge suspiciously consorts with the wife of Master Poynter. Neither the clock nor choir books are adequately repaired. The prior is violent and bad-tempered and on one occasion broke the clavichord (an early keyboard) of one of the brothers. Divine services are not performed as they should be according to the rules of the Order.

Bishop Richard

All this is most unsatisfactory. The flouting of Benedictine rules must cease. I will be instructing the Abbot to make sure that appropriate reforms are made and that this abbey conforms to the values of its saintly founder.

During the 19th century two Caen stone coffins were discovered under masonry at the entrance to the chapter house. They were the coffins of two monks covered with remnants of a piece of woollen cloth. In one coffin seeds of Valerian Rubra, the herb 'All Heal' were found and successfully grown into a plant which was exhibited locally. The seed was thought to be more than four centuries old.

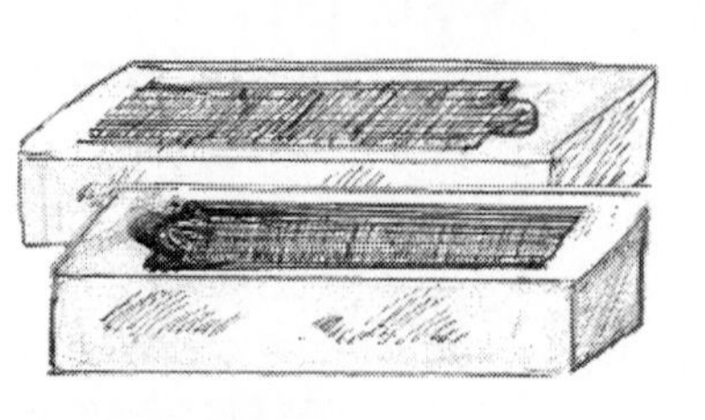

Stone Coffins

'All Heal'

The last years of Wymondham Abbey 1520-1534

The next visitation by the Bishop of Norwich in 1520 revealed further evidence of declining monastic standards. Many religious duties were being neglected like celebrating mass. Windows need re-glazing as pigeons were flying in and the bell towers and bells needed repair. Some sacred vessels, books and vestments were also found defective. Drunkenness and administrative laxity were reported. The Bishop ordered immediate improvements.

In the 1526 visitation the Abbot claimed all things had been reformed as instructed and all was well, but the Bishop found that choir books still needed repair, the novices required an instructor and monks were still guilty of lapses in behaviour.

By 1532 the Abbot and everyone questioned and examined by the Bishop agreed that all things were done as they should be. But by now it was too late. The wind of political change was blowing through the King's court and the future of the smaller monasteries was uncertain as Henry VIII sought ways to increase his income.

The last Abbot, Eligius Ferrers

Ferrers was a good preacher and it seems, a shrewd businessman, for just before the dissolution of the abbey, he leased Downham Hall manor his summer residence, to John Flowerdew, the King's agent in charge of the demolition at Wymondham. Ferrers secured a pension of £60-13s-0d, the stipend of Wymondham vicarage 1538-9 and later became Archdeacon of Norwich cathedral till his death in 1548. He was buried in the abbey church, perhaps beside the sanctuary.

Traditionally, the tomb of Eligius Ferrers in Wymondham Abbey

The dissolution of Wymondham Abbey 1536-9

Abbot and monks readily submitted to the Act of Supremacy in 1534 which made Henry VIII Head of the Church of England and removed the Pope's power. The abbey was closed in 1536 when four monks admitted sexual offences. In 1539 Flowerdew supervised the demolition of a building which had stood for nearly 400 years. But he was insensitive to the needs of the parishioners as he demolished the building with indecent haste keeping a large quantity of lead, for which the parishioners had paid, for his own use.

The seal on the stolen lead

Because the Abbot and his monks submitted to Henry VIII, they received pensions. Those who had worked on the abbey estate and tenants of the abbey lands now became subject to new lay landlords who bought the monastery lands when they came on the market. The chief casualties of the dissolution were local tradesmen who had supplied the abbey's needs and the lay workers such as scullions, cleaners, the laundress, barbers and certain ladies of ill repute! The revenue of the monastery was calculated at £263.18s.3/4d

The case for the dissolution of Wymondham Abbey was made by John Flowerdew

John Flowerdew, Sergeant-at-law

I live at nearby Stanfield Hall and have been appointed by the King's minister Thomas Cromwell to conduct the dissolution of the monastery in Wymondham. There are good reasons for this action. We live in changing times. England has broken with Rome and the Act of Supremacy demands that all the King's subjects pay allegiance to him not the foreign power of the Pope in Rome. Monks whose allegiance is to the Pope, cannot be true subjects of the King. In England the King and his Parliament are sovereign. Secondly, Henry VIII needs money for wars against our old enemies France and Scotland. So the abbey lands will be sold together with the stone, lead, slate, timber and glass. The monastery bells will be taken and melted down and then re-cast as cannons for the King's navy. Monastic wealth will be used for the benefit of the nation and as the monks co-operated, they will be fairly treated.

Finally, the evidence of moral decline and decay is rife here. The monks have been idle, drunk and neglectful of their religious duties; they have failed to keep the building in good repair and some have consorted with townspeople for immoral purposes. I am not a religious man, but I am certain that St Benedict would be ashamed of such behaviour.

For my part, I am glad to preside over the demolition of Wymondham Abbey. It has stood here for over 400 years but is a symbol of papal authority which has gone for ever. Now it too must go.

However, Flowerdew acted in a high-handed way during the demolition of the abbey. He misappropriated lead for himself, which had already been paid for by the townspeople, causing much bad feeling. His actions were not forgotten by Robert Kett and others. The feud between Kett and Flowerdew simmered and burst into the open again in 1549 when events at the annual fair brought the two men into fateful conflict triggering the outbreak of **Kett's Rebellion**.

Robert Kett, Wymondham's most famous son

Kett was born in 1492 and in time became a popular and respected member of the community. He was a small farmer, active in the life of the gilds and abbey church, and enterprising enough to become a tanner. It has been suggested by G Colman Green that Kett's tanyards used the lower water of the mill pond behind the Abbey after 1540. After the dissolution he acquired some monastic land and by the 1540s was a fully fledged yeoman farmer with some 50 acres of land and a number of properties including Gonville Manor.

Robert Kett

When our beloved abbey was dissolved, my brother William, myself and other parishioners petitioned to save part of the monastery building for the town. We were granted the steeple and bells (octagon tower), vestry, nave, south aisle, chapel of St Margaret and the Lady Chapel as well as Becket's Chapel. We were also allowed to buy timber, stone, lead and glass from the chapter house to build a new south aisle on the church. But that grasping lawyer, Flowerdew, interfered and we did not get all the lead we had been promised and paid for. Some say he has kept it for his own use; if so, it will not be forgotten.

I've lived in Wymondham all my life where I have farmed and kept a tannery. I served in the gilds and the abbey church along with my brother William. In 1539 after the abbey was dissolved, like many others I bought some monastic land which was put up for sale by the King's commissioner.

Now, ten years on in 1549, tensions are rising and there is much anger in Norfolk among the lower orders. They suffer much hardship because the great men of Norfolk are enclosing common land for sheep farming to further enrich themselves. This action deprives the poor of their livelihood on the commons. The Norfolk 'gentlemen' also abuse their power by denying the poor free use of forests and rivers, which have traditionally been used by all.

Flowerdew has pointed out that I have enclosed common land myself. This is true but only on a very small scale and I now realise such action is unjust for it deprives the innocent poor of their ancient rights. So I have pulled down my fences on the Fairland. Now I am ready to lead the poor commons if they will have me as a leader, to protest against injustice in this county. I say to the poor, 'Be of good comfort and follow me in defence of your common liberty.'

John Flowerdew

You, Master Kett are supposedly a man of property and yet you are ready to lead a mob of commoners in illegal action and betray the landowning class. It were better if you kept to tanning!

Kett

Don't lecture me Flowerdew - did you not despoil our abbey church and line your own pockets with the profits? Now you enclose common land at Hethersett causing misery to the poor there. We will appeal peacefully to the King to restore good governance in Norfolk. What we want is liberty and an equal use of all things. The power, covetousness and greed of the landlords knows no bounds and must be checked in the name of justice.

Flowerdew

You will regret your action; this madness will end in tragedy. You are the bane of Norfolk and I vow you will become the captain of fugitives.

Kett

I fear nothing from your or your threats, Flowerdew. Those who follow me are the King's Friends, seeking redress against unjust laws and oppression by the great men of this county who steal the commons from those who labour for them. Christ Himself will see we fight for simple justice.

For my part I am ready to sacrifice my substance, yea, my very life itself, so highly do I esteem the cause in which I have become engaged. We will appeal peacefully for the King's support against the abuse of their power by the local gentry. I will do nothing but what belongs to the duty of a true subject of the King. I pray that the protest that begins here in Wymondham will bring justice to the poor commons.

Flowerdew

Such action threatens the good order of society. Not all can be free.

Kett

Everyone has some rights surely and the order you talk of is a privileged one controlled by the powerful and greedy. We are the people of Norfolk who seek a better day for the poor. We have found a voice and will be heard. We will march to Norwich from the old oak on the highway. We will have these things, otherwise our protest and our lives may be ended together.

Kett's oak still stands by the side of the old Norwich Road, protected by iron railings.

The outcome of Kett's Rebellion 1549

Kett's march to Norwich resulted in a great camp on Mousehold Heath where 15,000 from all over the county were kept in good order for six weeks. However a petition to the King asking for social and economic justice was rejected. Eventually Kett's followers were defeated by a large royal army led by the Earl of Warwick and 3,000 rebels died at Dussindale. Kett and his brother William were found guilty of treason and in December they were hanged, Robert at Norwich Castle and William from the west tower of the abbey church which both men had loved and served so well.

'Kett's Castle' on Mousehold Heath

A Royal Visit 1573

In one of her many tours of the realm Elizabeth I spent some time in this part of Norfolk in 1573 and briefly visited Wymondham.

Elizabeth I

We are pleased to visit the fair town of Wymondham in our shire of Norfolk. However, while staying at my lord Wodehouse's seat at Kimberley Hall we were astonished so see a ghastly apparition hanging from the tower of your fine church. We are told it is the remains of one William Kett, the rebel, who with Robert Kett and others did take up arms against my brother,Edward VI, in 1549. This spectre must be removed for it is unfitting that a church should have been used as a place of execution.

The rebellion of 1549 led by the Kett brothers of this town is long over. For my part I believe that the unity and good order of this nation, England, must now prevail. Upheavals, divisions and rebellions of the past must not detract from the duties of all my subjects to be loyal to their Queen who values their loyalty and love above all things.

As a sign of this love for you it is our wish to grant the parishioners moneys to repair the chancel of your church, part of our national Church of England.

It has come to our notice that certain new religious ideas are afoot which do not conform to our English Church. But I do not want to make windows into men's souls; rather I would have them true to England and loyal subjects of their Queen who values their loyalty and love most highly. Such qualities will be sorely needed as the growing power of Catholic Spain threatens this Protestant realm and our interests in the new world of America.

Farewell my good people of Wymondham - the manifestations of your love will long remain with me a happy memory.

PART THREE

THE STUART CENTURY 1603-1714

The Great Fire of 1615

On 11 June 1615 a fire severely damaged 300 houses in the town. The value of the estimated loss was nearly £15,000. The areas worst affected were Vicar and Middleton Streets and parts of the Market Place and Bridewell Street. Among the buildings destroyed was the ancient Market Cross. However, a new Market Cross was built in 1617-18 as a result of the determination of the townspeople supported by Sir Henry Hobart.

Sir Henry Hobart (1554-1625) and the Market Cross

My family is from Suffolk and my profession is the law. In 1613 I was proud to be appointed Lord Chief Justice of the Common Pleas in London, where I have close links with very important people including the King's chief minister Robert Cecil. In 1616 when I bought Blickling Hall, I acquired much land in Wymondham.

Hobart's coat of arms from Blickling Hall

One of my properties, Grisaugh Manor with its jurisdiction over Wymondham market, gave me some influence in the town. The lamentable fire here in 1615 caused by malicious and wicked persons of evil disposition, greatly disturbed me. The losses in houses and goods were considerable and such a terrible event deserves every effort to help the town recover.

I requested that the Market Cross a particularly sad loss, should be rebuilt, as it is a focal point of the market and a symbol of local pride. Despite difficult circumstances a new building was completed in 1618, due to the energy of the townspeople. I came to Wymondham to admire the new Cross, and was made most welcome being entertained with wine, sugar, beer and cakes. Apparently a wealthy yeoman, Philip Cullyer, lent the sum of £25.7s for the rebuilding.

Some months later, however, I was petitioned by my tenants in the town who complained that some of my officers were planning to build shops on the market place around the new Cross creating a blemish upon it and the market place and leaving no room for cattle or for people to walk in the open space. Such action would leave no room for the main purpose of the market, namely selling livestock. I promptly reassured the town by dealing with the officers so that they could not cause any more problems to the market place.

So out of the ashes of the Great Fire, rose a fine new Market Cross which is a joy to behold. Surely it will continue to be enjoyed and admired by future generations of townspeople and visitors alike.

The importance of Wymondham Market Cross.

It was used for sessions of the market court where offences against the rules of the market were punished. The clerk kept a bell which he rang to open and close the market on Fridays. People buying or selling goods outside market times would be fined. Money was collected at the Cross for market tolls and stallholders fees. Licences of traders were inspected here and two constables kept order on market days.

A variety of other events also took place at the Cross - sermons were preached, royal proclamations made, laws published and criminals punished such as whippings of inmates of the local Bridewell. In 1713 a gallows was erected by the Cross and two men were executed for robbery and murder. Their bodies were then hung in chains on the gibbet on Norwich Common.

Beggars appealed for Christian charity by the Cross, banns were published, funerals paused so mourners could pray before going on to the abbey church. In Victorian days, men and women seeking employment lined up here hoping to be hired as labourers or domestic servants. However, the advent of railways in the mid 19th century led to a decline in the market. As a result, more use was made of the upper room of the Cross which served as a reading and news room between c. 1870 and 1912.

The carvings on the beams are representations of spoons and spigots, emblems of the wood turning trade, a staple trade in 17th century Wymondham and for long a major craft in the surrounding villages.

Wood Turning in Wymondham

The ancient craft of wood-turning was first noted in Tudor times. It flourished as a major industry in the town for some 300 years along with weaving, farming and brewing. Wymondham adopted the crossed spoon and spigot for its arms in the 20th century.

Though a humble craft, some turners became very rich like Henry Colman the Elder who left a new mansion, 4 acres and several closes and bequests of £25 in 1624. Robert Blome left lands and tenements in 1644 to his wife for the education and maintenance of their three children.

Why did wood turning flourish here? There were plentiful supplies of wood and timber in the area and a ready market in nearby Norwich. Blomefield refers to the fame of the town for wooden goods which employed men, women and children in their production. However, decline set in during the 19th century when the remnants of this ancient craft were absorbed by the brushmaking industry. Blomefield believed that like weaving, wood turning was an 'an innocent employment and better than idleness'.

The first House of Correction or Bridewell - 1619

The first prison in Wymondham dates from 1619. A medieval merchant's house which had stood on the site since about 1350, was adapted by the town authorities to include a dungeon. There are several references to this first Bridewell in the Town Book. This Bridewell survived until the late 18th century when, following the visit of prison reformer John Howard, a new Bridewell (the present structure) was built.

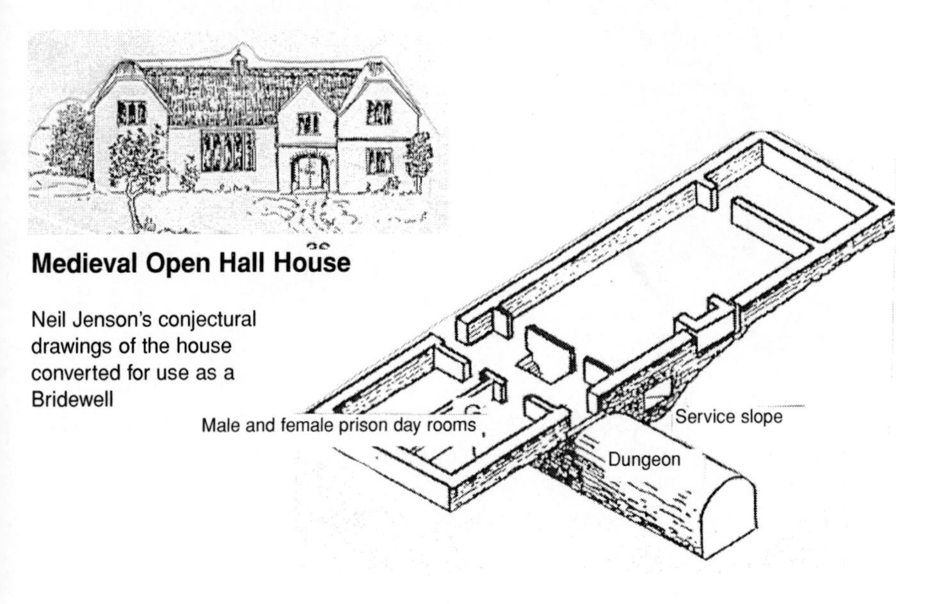

Medieval Open Hall House

Neil Jenson's conjectural drawings of the house converted for use as a Bridewell

The Civil War - Cavaliers and Roundheads 1642-51

During the political and military struggle between Crown and Parliament in the mid 17th century, counties, towns and families experienced divided loyalties. In Wymondham there was much sympathy and support for the Parliamentary cause. Two of the greatest landed families in the area, the Hobarts and Wodehouses, also supported Parliament. Wodehouse was also a critic of the King's archbishop Laud, whom he described as 'Loud organ Laud'.

However in nearby Ashwellthorpe lived the Knyvett family, staunch supporters of the King.

Sir Thomas Knyvett, supporter of the King

Ashwellthorpe Hall

My family is among the oldest in Norfolk. I live at Ashwellthorpe Hall. When the war started in 1642, I immediately declared for King Charles, unlike certain members of my class, namely the Hobarts and Wodehouses who betray the King by siding with those who would subvert the fundamental laws of this realm.

In 1643 I was at Lowestoft with others loyal to the King fortifying that port against Parliament. Then a Colonel Cromwell arrived with a large troop and we had no choice but to surrender to secure our lives. This same man had been in this area a year before being met outside Wymondham by 200 sympathisers from Norwich and this town. Then other parliamentary soldiers, stirred up by seditious puritanism, passed through Wymondham and pulled down the organ in the abbey church.

I was taken prisoner at Lowestoft and my estate, lands and rents were sequestered by parliamentary agents for their advantage. This was brute force not legal action. My family and I suffered greatly during the conflict which beset this kingdom. I was imprisoned at Cambridge and later Windsor Castle. When I was released my fortunes were beyond repair and England was a republic. Such was the fate of those who stood against regicides and republicans. Cromwell is the real 'man of blood' not the saintly Charles of blessed memory. Some fear that Parliament will give power to the common people who neither recognise our lineage nor accept that the gentry are the natural ruling class.

I hope I will live to see monarchy and true religion restored and the infamy of republicanism, military rule and puritanism overthrown. When I die, let this be my epitaph:

'Here lies Knyvett, who hated anarchy
Lived a true protestant, and died with monarchy'

In fact he died in 1658, the same year as Cromwell; he did not live to see the return of monarchy in 1660. He and his wife were buried in Ashwellthorpe Church.

Among the many in Wymondham who supported the parliamentary cause was a man who served in Cromwell's army.

Richard Wildman, supporter of Parliament

I was born and bred in Wymondham and a tanner by trade.When the war began, I was too young to fight but my chance came in 1645. I had always loved to ride horses and had made harness for them so I volunteered for Captain Swallow's Maiden Troop. This was part of the 11th Horse commanded by Edward Whalley and I found I now belonged to Oliver Cromwell's 'new model' army, known as the Ironsides; I'm sure you can guess why!

I was proud to be in Parliament's army against the King who has chosen to ignore the laws of this land. There's others like me in Wymondham, angered by King Charles' illegal taxes, who think the same. Anyway our army won great victories at Naseby and Langport - we were fearless in battle and Cromwell told us 'God made the enemy stubble to our swords'. I like soldiering and was well trained, fed and equipped.

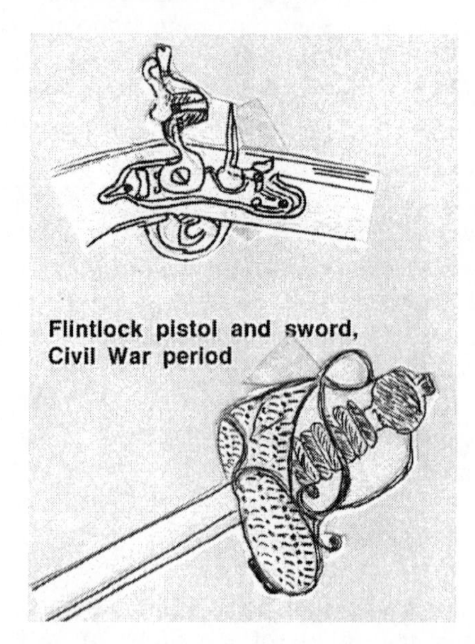

Flintlock pistol and sword, Civil War period

I stayed on after the King was defeated and served in the victorious campaign against the Scots in 1651. Then I was sent to a garrison at Ruthven Castle in the Cairngorms which was a bit dull. By 1655 I had been in the troop for 10 years and General Lambert told us we were one of the best regiments. I've seen the defeat and execution of the King in my lifetime and now it seems the world's turned upside down as Parliament rules the land.

Elizabeth Wildman

My dear husband died suddenly in 1655. Later I heard from a court in Norwich that I would be paid £3 towards maintaining our three children as Richard had lost his life serving the state. This makes me sad, but very proud.

In my husband's will I was left some money, arrears for his military service in Scotland, and I was to raise what I could from the sale of his pistols, saddle and bridle. He was so proud of these but I have to do this to help my family. Richard helped to give Parliament the victory but I do wonder if the troubles are really over.

Religious dissent in Wymondham

Apart from its parliamentary sympathies, Wymondham was also a centre for religious nonconformity. Various forms of Puritanism flourished in the town - Congregationalists, Baptists, Independents and Quakers. One of the most significant figures in these decades of religious turmoil was :

John Money, a notable Wymondham Puritan

I graduated from Cambridge and was ordained a priest in the Anglican Church in 1633. At this time new religious ideas were spreading which challenged the teaching of the Church of England. I became convinced that the church should be reformed and bishops' powers abolished. I believed that I should simply preach the Word of God as set out in the Bible. Bishop Wren of Norwich was persecuting reformers and people who thought like me. Many fled in the 1630s including James Gedney and Stephen and Thomas Gooch of Wymondham, who went into exile in Rotterdam, setting up an English church there.

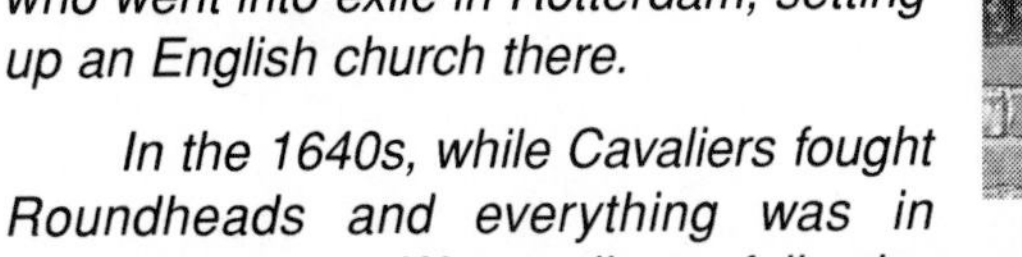

In the 1640s, while Cavaliers fought Roundheads and everything was in ferment, many Wymondham folk demanded reforms in the church, especially good preaching. The congregation was dissatisfied with the vicar, Joshua Meen. I loved preaching which came naturally to me; it was as if God was speaking through me. Anyway, I was asked to preach in the abbey church twice a week and was paid for doing so.

In time I also got involved with the religious refugees who returned from Europe to set up Independent and Congregational churches in Norwich. Some wanted to start such a church in Wymondham and I became the pastor of this group in 1652, though I was still preaching at the abbey.

When the monarchy was restored in 1660 new laws were passed to try and suppress these congregational churches but I refused to return to the old ways obeying bishops and suchlike. I believed that the power of each church is vested in the congregation itself and that independent judgement based on conscience and bible reading must prevail. I was evicted from my living for such beliefs, but I continued to preach at the home of Tom Osborne and sometimes hundreds of poor and gentle folk came to hear me.

The government tried to destroy these new independent churches but the Wymondham conventicle I founded was widely supported in the town. Now in the year 1672 Charles II has said preachers like me can have a licence to preach. We are allowed to worship in any building and manage our own affairs now. This is something Charles I tried to stop, Cromwell permitted and Charles II has finally legalised. It is good that no man shall be disquieted or called in question for differences of opinion in matters of religion which do not disturb the kingdom.

John Money died in 1673. In 1715 his supporters including Roger Gay, built a meeting house on land near the Fairland. It was one of the first independent churches to have a proper building. Money's epitaph reads:

'Eminent for his learning and piety and admired for his fervent, frequent and exact preaching ; and the rather because he never put pen to paper for his sermons, but wrought all in his head'.

The Legacy of the Civil War in Wymondham

In 1649 when Charles I was executed and many thought the wars were over, the impact of the civil war on the town financially and socially, was made clear by the Town Reeve, a descendant of Robert and William Kett.

Richard Kett, Wymondham Town Reeve 1649

The civil war has hit Wymondham badly. The town has paid a high price for the conflict between King and Parliament. Even before the fighting began, we faced new taxes when Charles introduced the hated 'ship money' in 1635. In Wymondham this amounted to £81.15s - only Norwich, Lynn and Yarmouth paid more than this.

This royal tax angered the townspeople because the King had not secured the consent of Parliament. When the war started we supported Parliament but we had to pay further heavy taxes from 1642. Then in 1645 another demand was made for us to give more money for Cromwell's New Model army. We did this and provided apparel and weapons to those of our menfolk who became soldiers. Some who enlisted in the parliamentary army were killed, while many others returned home badly maimed. The sight of limping men on Wymondham's streets is common now.

Now the fighting is over, the King is dead and Parliament is victorious but many families face tragedy and hardship. The Town Book shows that Wymondham has helped 124 men maimed in battle. It has also given support to the widows and children of 15 of our men who were slain fighting for Parliament. Between 1642-8 we paid out £43 2s 9d compensating wounded soldiers and in some cases provided payment for up to five weeks while they recovered from their wounds. We also helped 30 or more Irish folk who came here to escape the horrors of the Irish Rebellion. Others who have fallen on hard times during recent years and who passed through Wymondham, have also been helped by the town, such as three widows from Southampton plundered by Cavaliers who slew their husbands.

Here, let me read to you some extracts from the Wymondham Town Book which records payments made by the town authorities to victims of the Civil War.

Given to 2 Irish gentlewomen with 4 children whose husbands were burnt by rebels	*1s-0d*
Paid for a sheet for a poor soldier who died homewards as he came through the town	*2s- 6d*
Given Mrs Carr who lost her husband and all she had	*2s-0d*
Given Mrs Johnson and her 2 children, her husband slain	*4d*
Given 4 maimed soldiers returning from the army	*1s-0d*
To Arthur Sadd's wife, her two children likely to starve because her husband has gone to the army	*3d*
Paid Mr Ballister towards apparreling of soldiers who went with Capt Harvey	*£4-0-4d*
Paid 3 soldiers that went away with Capt Harvey	*£3-10-0d*
Given Mrs Seamore and 11 children stripped by rebels in Ireland and her husband slain	*1s - 0d*

PART FOUR

THE 18TH CENTURY AND BEYOND c.1700-1850

The 18th century - prosperity and progress

After the disasters and turmoil of the 17th century, Wymondham recovered to enjoy a period of growing commercial prosperity and further progress in agriculture resulting from the fertile soil of the area. Nathaniel Kent described the common land around Wymondham as equal to the finest in Norfolk and worth 20 shillings an acre, capable of serving as either good pasture or producing corn, hemp and flax. William Cobbett also commented on the good quality of the plentiful wheatfields. In the more settled conditions of the 1700s, the weekly markets and thrice yearly fairs flourished.

Turnpikes, transport and trade

In 1695 the first turnpike in Norfolk, perhaps in England, was established between Wymondham and Attleborough. It was extended to Hethersett in 1708. A memorial pillar to Sir Edwin Rich, who gave £200 towards the repair of this highway, was erected on the left side of this stretch of road near Dial Farm. This local turnpike brought great commercial benefits to the town. Trade became brisk as a straight road with better surfaces increased usage.

However, the main period of turnpike development in Norfolk came after 1770. This led to a demand for regular, reliable transport by coach and carrier. The golden age of the stage coach (1780-1830), brought further benefits to Wymondham. Weary travellers wanted regular stops on their uncomfortable journeys, so there was a need for more inns and alongside these associated trades grew up in the town, like wheelwrights, blacksmiths and harness makers.

By 1836 three coaches ran daily between London and Norwich calling at the 'Griffin', 'White Hart' or 'King's Head' en route. In addition local carriers like Sam Crow took goods from the 'Rose and Crown' in Damgate to Norwich on his horse and cart. Henry Johnson carried goods from Attleborough to Norwich, calling at the 'Rising Sun' in Damgate on the way. On Norwich market days carriers took Wymondham goods there three times a week. Wymondham also enjoyed road and carrier links with Hingham,

Dereham and Rocklands. The fruitful links with Norwich lasted until the mid 19th century when the coming of the railway dealt a body blow to the Wymondham market.

The King's Head, Wymondham's premier coaching inn, stood in the market place on the site now occupied by Woolworths.

New buildings in the 18th century

The new roads led to more buildings along them such as in White Horse Street and Norwich Road with the imposing Bridewell. Though the architectural make-up of Wymondham is largely rooted in the 16th and 17th centuries, some significant buildings date from this period. The handsome Bridewell was completed in 1785; on a different scale the growth of weaving in the town led to further expansion in Cock Street, Pople Street and Rattle Row. The most distinctive and distinguished domestic house in Wymondham, 16, Vicar Street, was built in 1793, while the largest, Cavick House on the edge of the town looking towards the Abbey, dates from the early 1700s.

Cavick House

16, Vicar Street is on the right

Along Middleton Street other important houses appeared - the Council Offices, Beech House and Caius House, complemented by the Georgian facade of the Priory, part of the old grammar school.

Caius House, now Jarrold's shop – about 1900

Weaving in Wymondham

The ancient craft of weaving has its roots in the Middle Ages when wool was the 'golden fleece' of the economy. In Tudor times enclosure for sheep farming became very popular among landowners. By the 17th century weaving was an important part of Wymondham life. John Middleton, a wool draper, left a will valued at over £200, a considerable sum at that time.

The golden age of Weaving in Wymondham 1740-1840

By the mid 18th century, weaving and cloth making carried out mainly by men, flourished in the town. Robert Cremer, Vicar of Wymondham, conducted his own census in 1747 which showed there were 155 weavers in the town. By 1780 weaving was the main employment. But the golden age of the Wymondham handloom weaver lasted for barely a century, though at its peak between 1780 and 1836 there was an extensive market for woven products in Europe and America. During the weaving boom, the town expanded further and Rattle Row, a terrace of weavers' cottages, was completed in 1820. Further development occurred along White Horse Street.

Weavers' Cottages in White Horse Street

The weavers lived in one or other of these

streets or Damgate, Friarscroft or Chandler's Hill. The population rose from 3,567 in 1801 to 5,485 in 1831. By 1836 there were 600 looms according to Whites Directory. The constant clacking noise of the weaver's shuttle echoed through the town during these years.

Most women had a spinning wheel and many produced yarn for Norwich weavers or sold reels in the market, especially in the early 19th century. Samuel Bignold, who later had a weaving 'factory' behind No. 58, Damgate, founded the Norwich Yarn Company.

The Weaving 'Factory', Damgate

For a time Wymondham, Norwich and Kidderminster were the only places in England where bombazines (silks) were made, until the Industrial Revolution reached Yorkshire. Other cloths were crepes, paramettas (light dresses of wool and silk, later cotton) and satins.

Strict regulations governed the production of yarn and cloth. Inspectors discovered much abuse such as 'false reeling' (short lengths) during the French Wars 1793-1815, when times were hard for many. Fines were imposed on offenders and in 1805 three local women Susanna Bond, Mary Minns and Susannah Goodings were convicted of 'false reeling'. Mary Walpole refused to pay her fine and was sent to the Bridewell. Others found guilty of this offence were: Delia Claxton of Attleborough, Elizabeth Cane of Braconash and Mary Ragg of Tacolneston. Some offenders were widows facing difficult times during the wars, like Elizabeth Harrison of Wicklewood. Judith Thompson was sent to the Bridewell for stealing weaving apparel in 1807.

The decline of weaving

The cloth industry in Wymondham was based on the 'domestic system' carried out in the homes of the weavers on their cumbersome and noisy looms. By the 1840s, however, the Industrial Revolution with its steam-powered machinery and factory production in northern England spelt ruin for the Wymondham weavers, early victims of the new industrial technology. Wages fell, unemployment rose and cottages fell into disrepair. By 1845 there were only 60 looms in the town. Strikes and riots by weavers were broken up by the 11th Lancers sent from Norwich.

In 1838 a Royal Commission advised parents to 'put their sons to anything but weaving!' Many embittered weavers supported the Chartist movement in 1841. Incidents of weavers embezzling materials in the 1860s were not uncommon when all seemed lost for these proud men. The fall in Wymondham's population from 5,485 in 1831 to 4,566 by 1881 reflected the depression in weaving. However, there was still a weaving warehouse in Town Green in 1869 (Cornelius Tipple) and a horsehair factory in Friarscroft Lane in the 1900s. Rattle Row remained as a symbol of the weaving era until it was sadly demolished in 1977, despite the efforts of the Wymondham Society to preserve it.

James Ball, a Wymondham weaver 1820-1902

Rattle Row

I was born in 1820 and started to use a loom when I was just a boy. I remember that Rattle Row was a newish street then and everyone living there was a weaver. There were hundreds of us weavers in them times; some say there was over 600 in 1836 when I was 16 years old. Of course every cottage had a spinning wheel used by the womenfolk. The clackity clack of our shuttles on the loom could always be heard around the town in those days - not anymore though.

By 1850 things was bad for many of us weavers; our wages fell and we couldn't keep our cottages repaired. You see by then machines, steam power, factories and suchlike in the north were driving us handloom weavers out of business.

While I was living in Frogs Hall Lane, I won a prize for a silk shawl I had woven. It was at the Great Exhibition at Crystal Palace in London in 1851. I was very proud and it shows that those machines still can't match the quality of us skilled craftsmen.

The government men told families not to put their sons into weaving. It was very sad but I kept going as it was hard to break a lifetime's habit. But as the years passed there was less and less looms around Wymondham. It's a shame when you consider there was once over 600 of 'em. Today in 1894, there's very few of us left. Why, many who used to be in weaving are now employed at the new brush works in the town. I'm too old for that - over 70 now and proud of the tradition of the handloom weavers.

The new Bridewell - 1785

There had been a House of Correction or Bridewell in Wymondham since 1619. By 1750 its underground dungeon had acquired a notorious reputation. In 1779 John Howard, the prison reformer, visited Wymondham during his national tour of English prisons.

John Howard

I first became acquainted with appalling prison conditions as sheriff of Bedfordshire. I decided to tour the country and produce a report on the state of English prisons with a view to their reform on the basis of humanity and efficiency.

When I came to Wymondham Bridewell, the Turnkey took me down eight steps to a dungeon some 15 feet by 8 feet and barely 6 feet high. The scene I witnessed was most disgusting with the prisoners - men, women and children in chains, in a darkened room and with hardly any straw on the floor.

The steps to the dungeon

John Howard (right) with the Turnkey

These dirty sickly objects were existing in the utmost squalor and only saw daylight on Sundays. I pointed out that keeping prisoners fettered underground had been illegal since 1774. The Wymondham Bridewell was one of the vilest prisons I visited during my tour.

I suggest the local justices build a new Bridewell based on the principles of reform, the tools of which are work, education and religion to rehabilitate the prisoners. Treated humanely, given separate cells, useful labour, moral instruction and firm discipline without the use of chains, prisoners will become better people. Brutal punishment is not the way to prepare them for a useful role in society when they are released.

After Howard's visit things moved quickly. In 1784 Sir Thomas Beevor of Hethel Hall and other local JPs began to plan a rebuilding, enlarging and fitting out of a new Bridewell. It was based on Howard's ideas and would keep prisoners secure but treat them better. This new Bridewell became a symbol of an orderly community.

Sir Thomas Beevor

Firstly we repaired the old house which had served as a Bridewell for so long. Then we added two new wings, each of two storeys which would be the main cell blocks of the prison. These will have separate cells for each prisoner - 21 in all and men and women will be kept apart.Prisoners will not be fettered but usefully employed from dawn till dusk, wholesomely fed, given fresh laundry weekly and regular religious instruction. Finally, there is a mill house containing a mill for cutting logwood and beating hemp. This block completes a quadrangle enclosing a yard of some eighty by seventy feet.

The Mill House at the new prison

I am drawing up rules for the new prison based on the ideas of Mr Howard and hope that the inmates will become better, more useful people as a result of their stay here. I believe that regular employment removes the irksomeness and misery of solitary confinement and accustoms prisoners to the practise of industry which will better prepare them for society when they are released. Furthermore, I hope that this example may excite a like attention in other counties and that Wymondham Bridewell will become a seminary of industry not corruption and idleness.

Henry Cunningham, prisoner in the first Bridewell

They calls me Henry Cunningham. The turnkey will remember me well enough cos I was the first to escape from the old Bridewell while they was building the new one. It was 1784 and ye see, for a time, there was a small gap in an outside wall opposite Browick Road. So while the turnkey was having his supper, a mate outside made the hole big enough for me to squeeze through. So I took me chance and got clean away wearing leg irons and all! It was great to get out, for that dungeon where we was all kept was a rat-infested hole. I near starved to death down there. So I took my chance when it came - what man wouldn't ? They put a price on my head, five guineas for anyone who could recapture me, but they never did!

The new Bridewell was completed in 1785 shortly after Cunningham's escape. In time it became a 'new model' prison and was copied in many parts of northern England and America.

Thomas Johnson, Turnkey at the new Bridewell

I'm the Keeper of the new Bridewell which was built by Sir Thomas Beevor. In the first prison here were kept the dregs of society - men, women and children. I was told about one prisoner, Elizabeth Pulley, who started paying for her life of crime in that dungeon. She was a real 'bad un' and I heard she did more time in other gaols before being transported to Australia.

But things are different now since Howard's visit; he didn't like what he saw and made it clear. So Beevor and other justices built this new Bridewell and I'm proud to be part of what our founder called a 'model prison'. It's certainly different from the old place though I keep the discipline firm.

The prisoners rise at six for work, with a half hour rest for breakfast, an hour at noon and another at 3 o'clock. After supper they return to their individual cells for the rest of the day. We've got work rooms, sick wards and a millhouse for cutting logwood. Women are kept busy spinning.

Why, they even get clean laundry regular and have daily prayers. I suppose it makes em better people. Of course they don't wear leg irons now and the dungeon's gone. Most prisoners are well behaved but if anyone is difficult, a few days in the punishment collar or 'fiddle' as it's called, quietens 'em down! It's an iron contraption weighing about eight pounds which holds the prisoner's head down and fixes his hands in a praying position.

The Turnkey shows an Inspector the punishment collar in use

The rule of silence while they're in their cells has a good effect in making prisoners reflect on their sins. Their demeanour must always be humble - I make sure it is! A prison inspector came here last week and he seemed to be impressed with what he saw at the Bridewell. It makes me proud to think I am doing a good job here.

A Prison Inspector at the Bridewell c. 1812

Mr Johnson can be pleased with this Bridewell which I consider to be one of the best managed in England. The excellent rules provided by Sir Thomas Beevor ensure enlightened treatment of the prisoners and harsh punishment is rarely necessary. The extreme cleanliness throughout is impressive and the conduct of the prisoners deserves the highest praise. The prisoners' earnings show how well it is conducted too, for they exceed their maintenance. Some of the former prisoners here have established themselves in industrious callings and are now in business and of good character. All this reflects well on the prison governor.

In 1825 Wymondham Bridewell closed and all the inmates were transferred to the new county gaol in Norwich. However, for 30 years it had been an example of good prison design and management.

In 1832 it was re-opened as a House of Correction for women prisoners and a laundry for the Norwich County Prison.

Emily Greenfield, Keeper of the Women's Prison

I've been in charge at the Bridewell since it re-opened and Sheila Bryant the matron helps me in the work. At the moment there are 19 women and two 'base' children here. Their ages range from 15 to 80. We have thieves, vagabonds and vagrants and some 'lewd' women too who have their children with them. Unfortunately these particular prisoners shout abuse from their cell windows at people walking along the Norwich Road. Persistent offenders are punished by me with a spell in solitary confinement. We have two women awaiting transportation at the moment too. The matron keeps the women busy all day. They rise at 6 am and work for 10 hours, before returning to their cells at 9 o'clock.

Sheila Bryant, Matron at the Bridewell

My job is supervising the prisoners in the laundry and making sure they do their work properly. They use the courtyard to hang out and dry the washing. Other prisoners sew and make mats but none of them like to pick oakum, that is picking fibres from pieces of rope which are used to help seal the decks of ships.

The women are well fed here and get 24ozs of bread daily, two pints of gruel and sometimes meat and potatoes. Most of them in here are thieves, who have stolen clothes, small sums of money and the like. Hopefully though, hard work in here and daily prayers will help to reform them.

Emily Greenfield

The running costs of the Bridewell are considerable. Last year, 1837, £531.0.5 was spent to pay for food, salaries, clothing, coal, bedding and repairs and also transporting prisoners to the hulks before their voyage to Australia. But I firmly believe that the useful work, discipline and moral direction we provide here does help to reform some of our prisoners who will change their ways when they are released. This makes our work worthwhile.

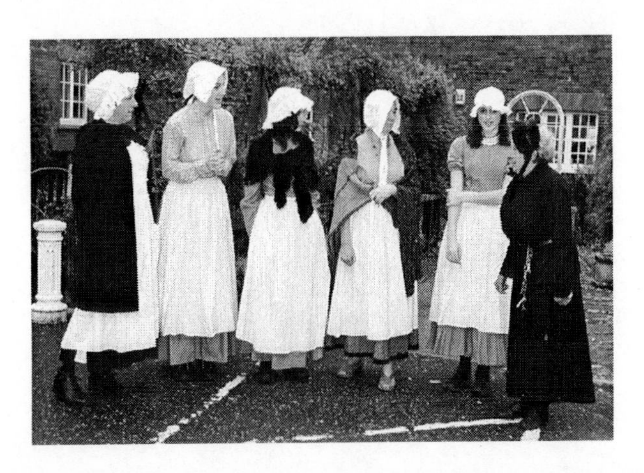

A group of prisoners with the turnkey and the prison matron

Many of the prisoners were women who had fallen on hard times and had no means of support, so in desperation turned to stealing.

Matilda Leaman, prisoner

I was sent here by the judge in 1842 for stealing things. But so would you if you was as poor as me. You want to know what I took - well, some combed wool, a cotton dress and some lace, not exactly the crown jewels eh? My friend took 4lbs of worstead picking and one shilling and sixpence. But we ain't ashamed cos them such as us don't have enough to put a rag on our backs sometimes, so we're forced to take from those who have more than enough in this world.

We can get bored in this prison sometimes, so we made a set of playing cards using single pages of a Testament folded twice to make a thick card. We sewed the edges with thread we took from the laundry when the matron wasn't looking. We used blood to mark the hearts and diamonds and charcoal for the spades and clubs. Mind you we had to take care we didn't get caught.

Some of us has been called 'lewd' women and our poor bairns 'base' children. But when a woman's desperate for food and clothing and is beaten by her man or master and gets paid nothing for her labour, is it any wonder she tries any means to get money in this harsh world. 'Lewd' is their word but our condition is by necessity not choice.

The Bridewell courtyard garden, formerly the prison yard

Mary Culpit, prisoner

I stole a petticoat and other clothing but I was desperate for clothes to keep warm, cos the likes of me has rags most of the time. Last week they put me on bread and water - for what? trying to speak to a fellow prisoner that's all! What's so unchristian about that?

Mary Anne Hudson, prisoner

I've been in here for 3 weeks but there's worse to come for me, much worse. Ye see I had to work as a farmer's servant for nigh on a year. He kept me there against my will and treated me cruelly. I was desperate to leave him so I thought if I fired one of his haystacks, he'd be so angry he'd let me go back to my family. Instead I was brought here to the Bridewell where I spend all day working in the laundry; but at least I get fed three times a day with boiled potatoes and such like. It's better than I had on the farm. But yesterday I was given some terrible news. I am to be transported to Australia. I cried all night for I fear I'll never see my family again. I ain't no criminal.

From time to time a prison visitor came to the Bridewell to monitor the quality of its management and the condition of the prisoners.

Harriet Martin, prison visitor

When I came here in 1851 I found the cells to be rather cold. The punishment of 43 women in the past year, because they tried to speak to fellow prisoners cell to cell during the silent period, seems rather harsh; for such an offence prisoners have to forego one meal and in the worst instance are put on three days bread and water and no work. The diet of bread and gruel is neither appetising nor nutritious. It is good that a chaplain visits each week. But I noted with pleasure, that each prisoner earns from her work in the prison £29 a year, offsetting the cost of their maintenance which is £33. The ratepayers will be pleased with that. However, I trust that the authorities will take note of the concerns to which I have referred.

A prison visitor at the Bridewell

The Wymondham Bridewell served as a prison for 86 years between 1785 and 1878. It was briefly closed between 1825 and 1832

Distress, unrest and agitation 1810-1850

During these decades there was much hardship among the poor in southern England and East Anglia. This was the result of the French Wars, enclosure of commons and the coming of machinery in town and countryside. The Corn Laws of 1815, passed by a landowning Parliament to protect its interest by keeping corn prices high, put bread beyond the reach of the poorest. Trade depressions were common, unemployment rose and wages fell. A harsh penal code added to the woes of the rural poor.

As a result there were food riots, protests and machine-breaking by Luddites. In 1827 a Wymondham handloom weaver was reported damaging a new power loom for silk at Ashwellthorpe valued at £1,000. He was lucky to escape with a fine of £50 and bound over to keep the peace. The machinery of the Industrial Revolution had hurt the weavers. Now the agricultural workers, already suffering from wage reductions, were hit by the new threshing machines which reduced jobs. Many took to poaching only to be punished by repressive Game Laws.

Discontent reached a peak in 1830-31 with the Last Labourers Revolt. A feature of this agitation were the 'Swing Riots', named after a mythical 'Captain Swing' who signed threatening letters to farmers in an attempt to get justice. The 'Swing' may be a reference to the flail used in threshing as when used, the stick 'swings'; a grimmer explanation is that such desperate men were prepared to swing or hang for their activities. Many Norfolk farm workers were influenced by the radical William Cobbett, who had drawn attention to the injustice of the enclosure of commons which left, 'fat beasts but lean men'. One man told him, 'once I had a cow and some sheep, but an act of parliament has taken them away from me'. The 'Swing' rioters attacked threshing machines and burnt corn ricks. They were desperate measures by a starving class. Punishment was severe and during these years, 19 were hanged and over 600 imprisoned, of whom 480 were transported. Captain Swing and his followers certainly shook the confidence of the rural gentry. Afterwards wages rose in some parts but rural poverty remained and many farm labourers and their families ended up in the Wicklewood Workhouse with unemployed weavers. It was still bursting at the seams in the 1840s.

The 'Swing' Riots around Wymondham - 1830

In 1830 four local men were arrested and charged with arson attacks at Wattlefield and Park Farms. They were Tom Wells, Stephen Jackson, John Smith who held meetings to discuss politics at his house in Damgate, and Jeremiah Head. They were taken to Norwich gaol for examination.

The records show that none of these men were actually **seen** committing the offence. One witness saw Tom Wells 'in a huddle' with another man, while another who called out the fire engine to Robert Rix's Wattlefield Farm, saw no one. The corn ricks at this farm were destroyed by the time the fire engine arrived. A third witness said he saw John Smith walking towards Park Farm from his house in Damgate.

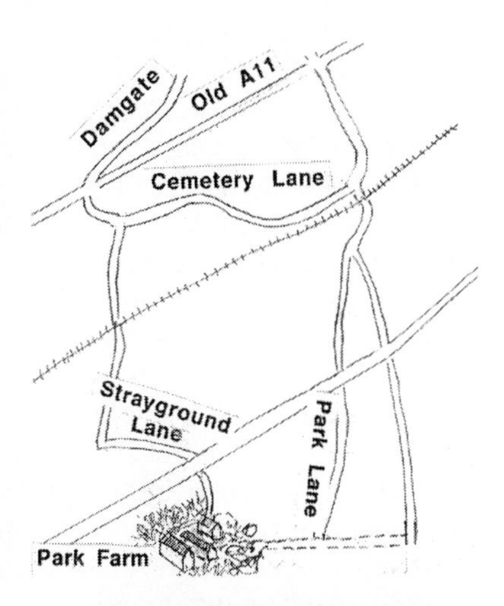

John Smith's route from Damgate to Park Farm, showing modern road names and railway

Stephen Jackson, farm labourer

There was four of us got arrested - for what? Rick burning at Park and Wattlefield Farms. But we bain't guilty. Any case I was at the Dove public house in Pople Street, then I went on to John Smith's house in Damgate. John was there from 3 o'clock and there must have been over 30 of us during the day. We was readin parliamentary acts and suchlike, hearing about William Cobbett and discussing politics and why we should have better wages. Tom Wells was there so was Jeremiah Head, Richard Kett, John Howes and others. So I knows nothin about any arson attacks.

Mind you, some of the gentlemen farmers are very unfeeling and brutal; they've brought us under the heaviest burden and into the hardest yoke we ever knowed. Those who rule the parish have robbed the poor of their common rights by ploughing up grass God sent, so the poor may feed his cow, pig, horse or ass. Why there's not more than a handful of 'em with all the land round here, whereas most of us are near starving. It ain't right.

We want better wages from those with the land and are rich enough - it's our labour that keeps them rich anyway. Then there's these threshing machines that take work from us; it's no wonder some have been smashed up.

Anyway these corn ricks they said we burnt - we did not and they took no notice of what we said to the constable and we was all taken to Norwich gaol. In the end only Tom Wells was charged but I saw him at Smith's house the night of the fire. None of them witnesses ever identified us and the constable came to me at 4 am and I told my wife I couldn't think what he wanted. He said I was an arsonist and it was no use denying it. That's the way the gentry work. Times is very hard for the likes of us farm labourers. Machines have robbed us of work and our wages are reduced. There will be more trouble unless something is done.

The confidence of the gentry was undermined by the activities of Captain Swing and his followers. The grand fabric of society rested on the broad rustic base of the rural labourers who had decided that they would tolerate injustice no longer without a fight. The disturbances of 1830 contributed to the reform agitation against the corrupt parliamentary system dominated by the landowners. In 1832 the momentous Great Reform Act was passed, a small step along the long road to parliamentary democracy.

The Chartist movement 1837-1848

The great trade depression in the late 1830s caused an increase in unemployment, high prices and low wages. The People's Charter was drawn up in 1838 setting out a programme for political reform including votes for all male adults and the secret ballot, together with a demand for economic and social justice for the working classes.

John Dover, a Wymondham Chartist

It was 1839 when there was a lot of meetings in Norwich supporting the Charter. Well, some of us had arranged for a Chartist speaker Rev Thomas Love to come out to Wymondham to address those interested. I issued handbills to announce the meeting which was to be in the market place, by the Cross. Well anyway, the authorities got wind of it all and the Lord Lieutenant called in the militia helped by the new police force just up from London. Everyone at the meeting was ejected to some six miles outside Wymondham along country roads. But later in the day Love returned and spoke to us about the People's Charter and the need for better conditions for working men and their families. All this was then condemned by Lord Kimberley, especially as our meeting was on a Sunday.

Kimberley Hall

Lord Kimberley said he would protect the people of Wymondham and their property from the idle and wicked and this Chartist scourge. He may mean well, but we Chartists think the poor need protecting from the rich and powerful. We're not afraid and we're not revolutionaries, but what we do want is reform of parliament, better working conditions, a living wage and such like.

I went to Norwich some days later with other Wymondham folk of like mind. There was lots of Chartist meetings going on there which we attended. It was quite an occasion and the dragoons was called in to clear us demonstrators from the streets - two got badly injured. There were Wymondham weavers at this demonstration too cos their cause had also been taken up by the Chartists.

Chartism continued to demonstrate the strength of working class opinion during the 1840s, especially in the towns, but it was also well supported in rural areas.

PART FIVE

VICTORIANS TO WORLD WARS AND BEYOND

The Police arrive in Wymondham

In 1829 Sir Robert Peel created the Metropolitan Police. It was so successful that soon rural constabularies began to appear. Wymondham set up one of the first forces in Norfolk.

PC Heathcote, a Wymondham policeman

We first came to Wymondham in 1833. There was some disorder in the streets at the time, so the town paid for three constables who soon restored order. They came from London and were known as 'Bobbies' or 'Peelers' after our founder Sir Robert Peel. They had a lock-up or 'clink' in Church Street near Becket's Chapel where the stocks used to be in olden times.

In 1850 we moved into the Bridewell. It was still a Women's Prison then but we had a corner opposite Browick Road with a house for a constable and his family, together with three remand cells for villains who had been arrested. When the prison closed in 1878 part of it became a courthouse. Another part was adapted for our use - the police 'super' lived in the turnkey's house, a sergeant and his family lived in the wing opposite Browick Road, and in the laundry block of the women's prison, another police constable lived - that's where the hard labour cells were. This block became our lock-up. It was also a popular overnight stop for tramps who knew the kindly wife of our sergeant would always give them some rabbit stew!

We had all sort of cases in the station - this 'ere rascal, not 12 years old , stole a rabbit costing a shilling. She was sent to prison for 10 days and then on to reform school. Then we had two lads of 7 and 9 who set fire to a corn stack. They were put in a cell for a night and then discharged by the magistrate - I think they got off easy. In 1852 another got 10 days for stealing a rabbit trap; the youngest vagrant in our station was five and he got 3 days in 1854. A woman was fined 2 shillings for stealing 3 camellias from Tom Standley.

But I felt sorry for the old man of 71 who got 10 days hard labour for stealing a beetroot worth a penny. Another man got 7 days hard labour for riding a waggon without reins.

As I said, there's been a magistrates court in the Bridewell too since 1879. This is very handy for us, cos when we 'book' someone, we put him in a cell, then next day take him before the 'beaks' in the same building!

The police station remained in the Bridewell until 1963 before moving into new premises opposite the Fairland. In 2001 the police moved again to the new County Constabulary HQ on the outskirts of the town.

The magistrates court started in the Bridewell in 1879, sharing the building with the police for over 80 years.

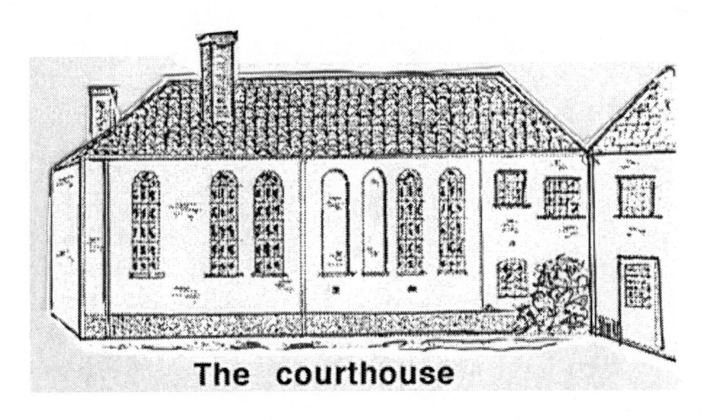

The courthouse

AA Bailey, a Wymondham magistrate

Before the court moved into the Bridewell in 1879, we magistrates used to have our sessions in the King's Head in the Market Place. The main courtroom in the Bridewell was in the former south wing of the prison which was converted for us.

During the 1880s and 90s we dealt with all manner of cases at the court here in the Bridewell. One man brought before us was charged with being 'drunk while in charge of a horse and cart'. Then we had those who tried to avoid paying their train fares at the railway station and parents who failed to ensure their children went to school. You see compulsory education started in 1881 and some families weren't too keen on it! We also had to deal with cruelty to children and animals. Routine business involved issuing licenses to sell beer and spirits and granting extensions to those organising harvest suppers.

At first all the magistrates were landowners, the most important being the Earls of Kimberley. Though the property qualification for magistrates was abolished in 1907, men from other walks of life have yet to join the bench.

We have a good working relationship with the police station and sharing the Bridewell allows for the efficient administration of justice. I believe that the courthouse is a symbol of a more orderly and civilised society around Wymondham.

The magistrates bench remained largely in the hands of the traditional ruling class until 1925. Gradually thereafter, people from all walks of life were appointed such as shopkeepers, teachers and office workers, so that the bench represented a fairer cross section of society. For example, Edwin Gooch who worked in his father's smithy as a boy and later became a Labour MP, joined the bench. In 1919 legislation deemed women competent to serve as magistrates. One of the first to do so in Wymondham was Mrs Alice Edwards of Old Hall, Barford in 1925. After the Second World War Mrs Ethel Gooch, wife of Edwin and a Labour Party activist, also became a magistrate. Jack Boddy was only in his twenties when he was appointed; he later became General Secretary of the National Union of Agricultural and Allied Workers.

The magistrates court continued in the Bridewell until 1992.

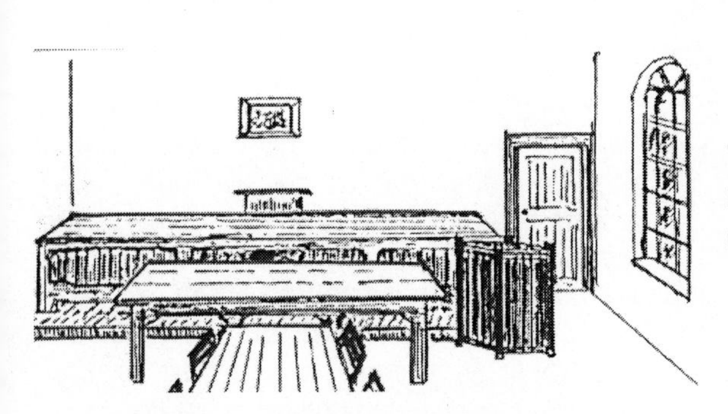

The main court room,now the main gallery of the museum

The coming of the railway

In July 1845 Wymondham Railway Station was opened. It was an important stop on the Brandon to Norwich line linking Norwich with London via Ely. The coming of the railway was a major landmark in Wymondham's history. It brought economic and social benefits, but the town's weekly market was never quite so successful again. The railway system expanded rapidly in Norfolk during the mid-Victorian years and in due course Wymondham station became an important junction.

Percy Cobb, Wymondham Station Master

My grandfather remembers the opening of the station in 1845 as a very important event in the town's history. A year later in 1846, we were linked with Great Yarmouth too and soon excursions to the seaside were available costing 3d (1p). These were very popular and hundreds took the chance for a day out to get some sea air.

Of course before the railway, the main transport was coach and horses on the old turnpike, but now their days were numbered. Nothing can compare with trains; they're fast, reliable and not too expensive. Some of the inns which had done a good trade with the stage coaches suffered, but the King's Head still flourished and organised horse-drawn cabs to meet each train. The town's mail is collected in a pushcart.

Wymondham station was duly linked with Dereham in 1847, Fakenham in 1849, Swaffham and King's Lynn in 1848, Ipswich in 1852 and Wells in 1857.

Then in 1862 the Great Eastern Railway (GER) started - that was when all the railways in the eastern region were amalgamated. The last line to be built to Wymondham was from Forncett in 1881.

So now we're really flourishing at the hub of things in Wymondham. I have over 30 people working under me at the station. There's foremen, porters, shunters, signalmen, level crossing staff, booking clerks, drivers and firemen, and of course staff for our refreshment room and the WH Smiths, bookstall. They look very smart in their uniform and they can always get a hot cup of tea during the quiet periods, though there aren't many of them!

Wymondham station

You can go to London on the railway for 1/6d. Briton Brush have their annual works outing on the train and they use the sidings track to send out their factory goods and bring in raw materials from abroad.

The farmers didn't like the trains at first but they soon realised that the railway opens up the countryside, linking it with other parts of the county and further afield. Now they can move their produce to market more quickly and animals are often passengers on the trains, though I've known goats eat through their destination labels! And of course we can now get fresh fish from the coast easily.

In 1923 the GER became part of the London & North Eastern Railway or LNER, so all the letters on the rolling stock were changed. In turn, the LNER was Incorporated in British Railways in 1948.

Brewing in Wymondham

One of the earliest records of brewing in the town is the will of Thomas Woodcock, a Wymondham brewer who died in 1593 leaving property valued at over £116 - a very good sum in Tudor times. However, it was not until the 1780s that brewing was established on a substantial commercial basis in Wymondham by the Stephenson family and especially John Stephenson Cann. In 1824 the business became Cann & Clarke and by 1850 it owned more than half of the town's 30 public houses.

Arthur Bailey, Manager of the Wymondham Brewery

As manager of the brewery I enjoy rent free accommodation in the brewery's mansion house facing Market Street. I am paid an annual salary of £500. Nowadays, that is in 1883, the brewery owns 21 licensed houses in Wymondham and over 80 throughout Norfolk. Local pubs we supply by horse and dray, but we use the railway to carry our beer to pubs further afield.

Our best selling beer is a mild ale which is equally popular with farm workers, railwaymen and weavers. I remember when they were building the new railways in the area. The contractor ordered 150 of our barrels over eight months. We delivered them to Eccles Station, happy to oblige thirsty railway workers with our finest ale.

We also produce fine Norfolk malt for the London breweries. We've got four maltings in Wymondham, one opposite the Cock, another opposite the Bridewell and two in Market Street.

We're a big employer in Wymondham now and our business in Brewery Lane stretches as far as the back of Wharton's butchers. Each day the horse and drays set off on their rounds going down Brewery Lane then around the pubs and up to the station. We've got 40 men working here doing different jobs - malsters, draymen, cellarmen, coopers who make and repair barrels and general labourers and clerks. They've got secure jobs too - there's always a demand for good beer!

The Wymondham Brewery 's large premises in Brewery Lane has to be well -organised to compete with the best brewers in the county.

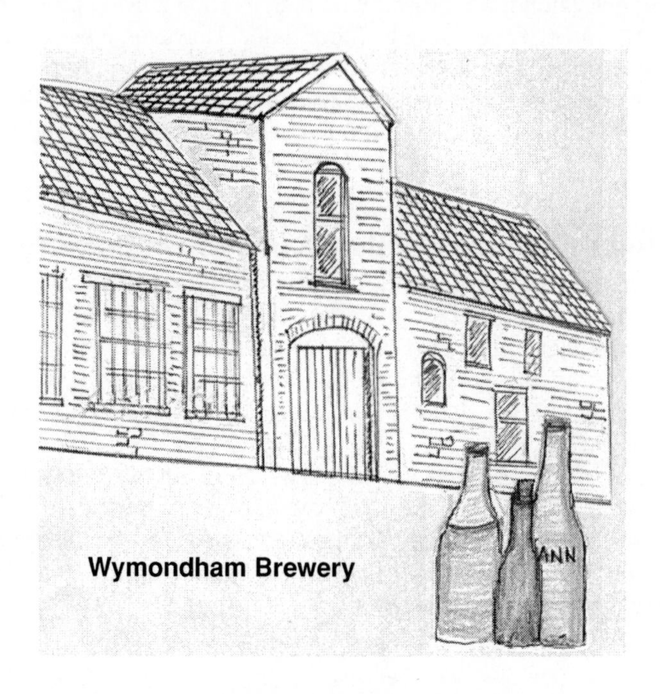

Wymondham Brewery

We look after our horses in good stables with a hayloft and harness room nearby. Then there is a malthouse, a cooperage, a scalding room where steam and hot water clean the barrels and casks. Finally, there's the office where I work. Cann's Brewery has come a long way since the first commercial brewers started in Wymondham in the 18th century. I'm proud of our reputation in the brewing business.

In 1894 Cann's Brewery was bought out by Morgans of Norwich and brewing in Wymondham came to an end. The maltings opposite the Bridewell were demolished and a row of houses called Elm Terrace was built. In 1931 the Brewery's huge beer vat was eventually converted into a swimming pool by William Smith.

Educational advances in 19th century Wymondham

The monks were the main source of education in the town during the Middle Ages though it was not widely available. Robert Kett, who was a friend of the last Abbot, was probably taught to read and write by the monks. A turning point came with the founding of the Edward VI Grammar School c. 1550, endowed from recently dissolved guild and monastic lands. The school building was Becket's Chapel. In 1672 Robert Dey left his house next to the Green Dragon for the use of the 'skolemaster' and his family.

By the 1830s a number of small charity schools had been founded, including one in Damgate.

The schoolmaster's house next to the Green Dragon

The next big step was when William Papillon, vicar of Wymondham (1788-1836), opened two schools sponsored by the Church of England National Society. He was a man of great energy and many interests apart from his religious work.

William Papillon - not just the Vicar of Wymondham

I have served this parish for nearly 50 years and as I look back on my ministry, I hope it will be seen as fruitful for the abbey church and also the wider community of the town.

I have always been conscientious in performing my church duties - services, sermons, social events, pastoral care and so on, but I have many other interests; a vicar should always have a broad outlook on things. Houses have always interested me and when I found that the vicarage was too small for my purpose, I had a fine new house built opposite in 1793 - it serves my many interests very well. Later on I acquired other properties in the town, including Cavick House on a short lease.

Secondly, I felt that the beauty and uniqueness of the Abbey meadows should be saved for posterity. I therefore set up the Papillon Trust to guarantee them in perpetuity.. The former abbey meadows which lie between the churchyard and Damgate form a historic and peaceful feature of our town. I believe such a haven of calm and serenity should be kept that way.

I was concerned for many years that the King's highway passes very close by the church walls and west porch. But, as a result of my efforts, the road is to be re-routed next year (1836). It will then pass a respectable distance from the church and the bustle of life outside, will not disturb the services within the ancient walls of our beautiful church.

Last year (1834), I was glad to be instrumental in the archaeological dig in the monastic ruins which led to the discovery of two lead coffins revealing more about the sad story of our founder's wife and child.

However, I am particularly proud of my contribution to the cause of education in this parish. The grammar school cannot meet the needs of all our children. So with the support of the National Society of the Church of England I have set up a school for 200 boys and girls in Church Street and an Infants school in Lady's Lane. If we are to liberate our children from ignorance and illiteracy, we must open their minds to knowledge and equip them with the means to learn and so lead more fulfilling and useful lives.

About this time (1835), the grammar school moved from Becket's Chapel to the Priory in Middleton Street; there is a fleur de lys over the door. The school remained there until it closed in 1903. Opposite, where Priory Gardens and the former Post Office building now stand, were the school's playing fields and fives courts. The headmaster here in the late 19th century was the Rev. Challis.

The Priory

Rev B Challis, Headmaster of the Grammar School

I'm proud to be in charge of this grammar school which dates back to Tudor times. Archbishop Parker founded a scholarship of £20 at his college Corpus Christi for two of our pupils native to this town. The school provides those boys with modest means an opportunity to develop their intellectual potential. We also have 60 boarders here who pay 30 guineas a year.

Boys work hard here especially in Mathematics, Latin and English. When the Principal of the Diocesan Training College in Norwich inspected the school recently, he remarked on the 'good tone', adding that the boys were 'imbued with a spirit for work'.

Our boys rarely misbehave. I find the cane is a useful and healthy corrective to disruptive behaviour. They know what is expected of them and I am pleased that many of our pupils have gone on to serve with distinction in public life such as in the army, church, business or public affairs.

Occasionally we have problems. Last week there was a snowball fight in the streets between our pupils and those from the Commercial School (opened 1886). While recognising the natural high spirits of boys, such behaviour must not happen again as it endangers others in the streets and damages the school's excellent reputation.

All the masters here are graduates of Oxford or Cambridge, members of the Church of England and qualified to teach Greek and Latin. So our pupils get a good grounding in the classics. The boys know they are privileged being educated at the grammar school where we insist on good manners. We aim to turn our charges into good Christian gentlemen who will make a useful contribution to society. The trustees keep me on my toes too. They can dismiss me if dissatisfied with my work. So I make sure that everyone is working for the good of the school. And now if you will excuse me I have some books to mark!

During Victoria's reign, further progress in education benefited many more children in the town. By the 1830s there were several small 'charity' schools. Following the National Schools initiative which Papillon actively championed, the educational society of the Nonconformist Churches, the British and Foreign Society, founded its first school in Fairland Street linked to the Independent chapel in 1843. In 1849 the National Society built a school for 40 children on Norwich Common, which eventually closed in 1935.

During William Gladstone's great reforming government (1868-74), 'education for all' was a top priority. Board Schools were to be built where there were insufficient church schools. In 1872 the new Wymondham School Board took over the Norwich Common school. In 1874, it built new schools at Spooner Row for 130 pupils and Silfield for 70 pupils. In 1876, Browick Road Board School for 560 boys and girls and infants was opened.

Browick Road School

The cost of these new schools was £1,223, £589 and £5,886 respectively. In 1886 the Commercial School was opened in the Congregational Church Rooms on the Fairland with 100 on the roll. It only lasted until 1898 but provided great sporting rivalry with the Grammar School.

The last school to be built before the Second World War was Wymondham Senior School (now the High School) in 1938. It was well equipped with assembly hall and stage, gymnasium, workshops, domestic and science laboratories and playing fields.

Brushmaking comes to Wymondham 1886

Brushmaking has had a long association with the town but the story begins in Norwich in 1746, when S D Page & Sons set up a business making baskets and brushes. Somewhat later in London, D Matthew & Son took over a brushmaking and wood-turning business in Tottenham which grew steadily from 1807-1870. These two firms amalgamated in 1922 to form the **Briton Brush Company** which became the most important brushmaking business in Wymondham.

The traditional craft of wood-turning in Wymondham became linked with the brushmaking industry. By 1836 wood-turning was virtually obsolete but a few individuals kept the ancient craft alive. Robert Semmence was the most important of these - a dish maker and bowl turner who also made spoons and cups from local timber. He also produced brush-backs, scythe handles and the like from his Cavick saw mills and turnery.

By the 1880s the Norwich brush industry in the Haymarket was expanding and Page wanted another factory to install new equipment, like the Gane filling machine, to increase production in an industry which only produced hand-made goods. Semmence was already doing business with Page supplying the Norwich factory with brush-backs. Then he helped Page purchase land in Lady's Lane, less expensive than in Norwich, where Page's new brush factory and sawmill covering several acres was opened in 1886. The Wymondham factory started to accommodate both the machine brush production and the wood working side of the business.

In 1896 Page acquired the former premises of Cann's Brewery in Brewery Lane. Here dyeing processes were carried out in the former vats and combing and cleaning of fibres for use as filling materials for brushes.

Soon the factory was importing fibres and bristles from India, China, Russia, Poland and Siberia.

By the end of Victoria's reign (1901), the brush works on Lady's Lane, where machinery had become firmly established, was a key element in the Page business. The first phase of the story of brushmaking in Wymondham was complete. Over 600 men and women were employed in the town and in Norwich and the foundations were laid for further expansion in the 20th century.

Semmence's sawmills and brush works to the right of the Abbey

Why brushmaking came to flourish in Wymondham

There were several reasons for this. Firstly, many people in the town and surrounding villages were unemployed at this time as a result of the agricultural depression and the decline of weaving, so the arrival of a new and dynamic industry was very welcome. Women too were willing to work in the industry. The local tradition of wood-turning and plentiful supplies of timber also contributed to this process. There was also suitable land for industrial development. Good rail links for importing raw materials and exporting the finished products also helped. Finally, S D Page was an enterprising company which bussed workers in to the factory from the surrounding villages.

Copy of a water colour of Page's Wymondham factory - early 1900s

Brushmaking in the early 20th century

During this period expansion continued as machinery revolutionised production. The Gane filling machine fixed tufts and bristles into the brush stocks and boards at a rate of 50 'knots' a minute. Vast numbers of shaped stocks (handles) were needed. By 1904, 30,000 poles for stocks and 750,000 brush-backs were in the drying sheds of Page's factory in Lady's Lane.

During World War One (1914-18), production was further stimulated and Page's made four million brushes for the armed forces. By 1917 a second brush making concern had appeared when CWS (Leeds) bought George Semmence's sawmills in Chapel Lane. From here, CWS supplied its Leeds factory with 'backs' and other wooden components. In 1922 Page and the London brush firm of D Matthew joined to form Briton Brush, a landmark in the story of brushmaking in Wymondham.

A group of brush workers from Page's factory 1909

A Wymondham street scene in the early 1900s

Women's struggle for the vote

Between 1832 and 1884, three parliamentary reform acts extended the vote to the majority of the male population, but women were excluded from this process. By 1901 women had made some advances in a male-dominated society. For example, they could be doctors, nurses, teachers, take university degrees and keep their own property after marriage. But they still had an inferior status in society, denied many things simply because they were women.

In the years before 1914 however, some women campaigned vigorously for equal political rights. Their leader was Mrs Emmeline Pankhurst who in 1903 founded the Women's Social and Political Union (WSPU) to campaign for women's suffrage or the right to vote. Her supporters were known as suffragettes. The suffragette campaign drew public attention to the injustice of the situation. In 1905 Mrs Pankhurst came to Norwich to speak on the issue of political rights for women. Among those present at this meeting, was Winifred Mayo.

Winifred Mayo, a Suffragette supporter

I have supported the WSPU since it started and last week I went to St Andrew's Hall in Norwich to hear Mrs Pankhurst speak on women's rights. Unfortunately, it was impossible to hear her - why? because she was howled down by disgraceful men and was even in danger of being injured. And men have the effrontery to say women are not responsible enough to vote!

*I am in Wymondham today to urge the women of this town to support the suffragette cause. Perhaps some of the men might join us too! We've been moderate and reasonable for some time now, but the indifference of the male establishment has led some of us to adopt more extreme methods to attract attention to our cause. They have chained themselves to railings, even broken windows. This is because we are fed up with being treated as second class citizens. The government claims it is too busy with more important things. But nothing is more important than women's political rights. Half the population has no voice or the same rights as the other half. Surely, it is wrong that all laws that affect women are made by men. Society seems to exist solely for men. Well, we plan to change all that. We're not law breakers but we simply want to become law-makers alongside the men. As you know, women already play a vital role in the home and some of us have become doctors, teachers, nurses and the like. But we demand and deserve to be treated as political equals with the right to vote. I urge the women and men of Wymondham, which has a long tradition of independence and fairplay, to join our campaign to persuade the authorities to support our aim: '**Votes for Women**'.*

Between 1905 and 1914, the Suffragettes became steadily more militant and even violent. They set fire to pillar boxes, broke windows and damaged golf courses. In 1913, Emily Davison sacrificed her life for the cause at the Derby. Many were imprisoned for their activities; they went on hunger strike and were force-fed. But despite some public sympathy, their efforts failed to change the government's mind.

The First World War (1914-18) transformed the situation. Women demanded the 'right to serve' as the men went off to fight. Many women worked in factories to support the war effort and took on all kinds of jobs traditionally associated with men such as in the armed services, munitions factories, as drivers, farm labourers, shop assistants and clerks. In recognition of their conspicuous and vital contribution to the war effort, women over 30 years of age were given the vote in 1918. Suffragettes continued to campaign until equal political rights were finally granted to all women over 21 on the same basis as men. This was granted in 1928.

World War One - casualties and the hospital at Abbotsford

The outbreak of the 'Great War' in 1914 had tragic and lasting consequences in Wymondham as it did throughout the nation. In the heady early days of the war, 750 volunteered to serve in the army. A further 450 joined when conscription started in 1916. Soon the scale and horror of the conflict became apparent as vast numbers of casualties arrived back in Norfolk at Norwich station. The Norfolk & Norwich Hospital had set aside 150 beds for the war casualties, totally inadequate for the huge numbers of wounded men who overwhelmed its resources. All the county hospitals were overstretched and more centres and temporary hospitals were needed.

In Wymondham the wounded were initially accommodated in the Vicarage Room in Church Street. Then Mrs Cautley offered part of her home Abbotsford, in Vicar Street, as a hospital. It had one ward and one day room.

The hospital ward at Abbotsford

A nurse's home was set up at nearby Turrett House

The commandant of the hospital was Mrs Martin-Jones, the vicar's wife. This Voluntary Aid Detachment (VAD) existed for four years. It had 73 Red Cross nurses during that period and over 800 wounded soldiers were patients there. Fund-raising kept the hospital going; the total cost was £6,000.

Among the visitors to the hospital was Sgt Maj Harry Daniels V.C. a Wymondham man who was awarded the Victoria Cross for 'conspicuous bravery' at the battle of Neuve Chapelle in 1915. He received a great welcome at Norwich station and a civic reception by the mayor of Norwich.

One of the Red Cross nurses at Abbotsford was Ella Wharton. She kept an autograph book which many of the patients signed. Sometimes they wrote more than just a signature:

Wymondham Red +
13/6/16

When the name that I write here
is dim on the page
And the leaves of this Autograph
yellow with age
Think of me kindly and do not
forget

I'll remember

Brief extracts from Nurse Ella Wharton's autograph book

When earth's journey here is ended,
And earth's paths are no more trod,
May your name in gold be written,
In the autograph of God

Are we winning, are we winning,
I sincerely hope its true,
All will be well, when we bid farewell,
To the trenches and bully beef stew

Dear Ella May, for you I pray,
May God his angels send-em,
To guard through life from pain and strife,
The sweetest maid in Wyndem!

Alas, that man has lost a leg,
Yet with a radiant face,
He walks complaisant on his peg,
With compensating grace.
But there goes one across the way,
Who needs compassion much,
He lost his faith in heaven one day,
For him there is no crutch

By 30 June 1915, 2,915 wounded soldiers in 28 trains had been conveyed from Norwich station to various hospitals like the one at Wymondham. These included 1,348 stretcher cases. By the end of October 1916, 123 convoys, totalling 12,023 wounded men returning from the trenches to 'Blighty', had been greeted by sympathetic crowds at Norwich station, before they were taken to a hospital. The Red Cross nurses played a vital role during this time of tragedy and pathos.

Pte Gudgeon, a patient at the Wymondham Red Cross Hospital at Abbotsford

I was brought here after being wounded at Neuve Chapelle. It was terrible out in the trenches.I saw some things I never thought possible on this earth. Amid the mud, noise of guns and barbed wire, we had to cope with trench feet and rats as well. And all the time, men with terrible injuries especially those caught in 'No Man's Land'. I was one of the lucky ones though cos when I was sent home to dear old 'Blighty', at least I'd still got all my limbs. Here in Wymondham I had a memorable stay. The nurses were marvellous to us – nothing was too much, though they wouldn't let us have a drink or a Woodbine except in the garden!

I remember one day particularly - it was when Sgt Maj Harry Daniels came to visit us. To think I was in the same sector at Neuve Chapelle as that great hero. Others have told me the fighting got worse after I left and what Harry Daniels did was really special. I felt honoured to have met someone who won the V.C. I don't like talking about the war - for what I saw doesn't bear the telling! We all hope and pray it will soon be over so that all our comrades can come home.

In the 'war to end all wars', 142 Wymondham men were killed and over 400 others were wounded. In November 1918, as part of a 'Feed the Guns Week', patients at the hospital who were capable of walking, joined a procession behind an 18lb gun drawn from the railway station and around the town. After the war there was a programme of 'welcome home' events in the town. But the most significant event was in 1921 when the War Memorial was unveiled and dedicated after a procession led by Red Cross nurses and including servicemen and ex-patients of Abbotsford.

Jane Bowden, a Red Cross nurse at Abbotsford

I remember going to Norwich station in 1914 to greet a convoy of wounded soldiers. They were truly a sorry sight, some had terrible wounds; some had crutches and one leg, some were too badly injured to walk and seemed to be almost totally covered in bandages. We made them feel as welcome as possible, gave first aid where appropriate and served coffee and milk to those who could take it. The largest convoy to arrive that day had 220 patients, including 146 on stretchers.

I worked at Abbotsford in Wymondham, one of the many new hospitals created to cope with the growing numbers of casualties. Our days were long and at night there was washing, cleaning, and starching to do as well as our nursing duties. The men had been badly battered in body and mind so we offered as much support and comfort as we could. They had borne the strain of trench warfare for months though few of them ever talked about it. I expect it was too horrible.

Despite their injuries some of our patients remained very cheerful and wrote comments in an autograph book. One man told me tearfully about 'No Man's Land' where he had tried to help a fallen comrade in the midst of battle and failed. These men must have endured a living hell. We felt privileged to look after them.

Sometimes there were special events for the patients. In 1916 we took ours to the Sports Day for Disabled Soldiers at Town Close on Newmarket Road. There were all sorts of races for the wounded soldiers and us nurses - blindfold boxing, a crutch race, a sack race, an egg and spoon race, a flat race for nurses, a musical chairs for the wounded, a comic costume race, a skipping race for nurse and two soldiers, a blindfold obstacle race where the soldier was guided by a nurse using string reins. That one was quite exhausting! It was good to see those poor men enjoying themselves and entering into the spirit of it all. I thought I would never see some of them laugh again after what they had been through. But that day took away their painful memories of the trenches for a time. It was all very moving.

The plight of farm workers and the Great Strike in 1923

Between 1890 and the outbreak of World War Two in 1939, the farming industry struggled to survive. By the 1920s it was at its lowest ebb in Norfolk because of foreign competition. Cheap imports of Canadian wheat, New Zealand lamb and Argentinian beef severely damaged Norfolk farmers. Wheat prices fell by 50 per cent between 1920-23 and wages fell to 22 shillings a week. Farmers wanted their workers to do an even longer working day. One farm worker who suffered at this time was Bert Hayzell of Attleborough; he started work as a crow scarer on Park Farm Wymondham and later became a horse-man looking after six horses seven days a week. Now his wage fell from 15 shillings a week to 4/6d by 1923. Such experiences caused widespread bitterness among farm workers leading to the great strike in 1923.

Farm labourers during the strike

Edward Hewitt, a farm labourer

I was glad we came out on strike - there was 10,000 of us they say and we were out for four weeks. We had to make a stand against wage reductions and longer hours. We've got families to feed too and we deserve a family wage. The farmers were bleeding us to death.

I went up to Wicklewood during the strike, because good ole George Edwards who founded our union was there. We marched down the High Street to Kimberley Park where Lord Kimberley welcomed us. He was the first Labour peer and he was very sympathetic to us; so was Edwin Gooch of Wymondham, a good man always working for us farm labourers.

George Edwards and Edwin Gooch with strikers in Wicklewood

We were desperate then and at the demonstration in Kimberley we demanded higher wages, no increase in hours, and food from the Guardians of the Wicklewood Workhouse to relieve the hardship of many families. Some strikers ended up before the magistrates at the Wymondham Bridewell - some justice! We thought we were winning when hundreds of police came and the farmers were worried on account of no spring corn being sown.

Anyway after the strike we did gain something - a return to wartime wage levels of 25 shillings, there would be no increase on our hours and no victimisation of the men who had been in the strike. Our numbers, and the support of Edwards and Gooch ensured the plight of the farm worker was made public and clear. But some men lost their jobs because of the strike. That's not right and it's no wonder many remain bitter .

The 1923 strike was important in terms of scale and it halted the farmers' attempts to cut wages further and lengthen hours of work. The union which Edwards had founded and Gooch was to become president of in 1928, gained experience and confidence and thereafter played an important role in negotiating for farm workers in future years.

Edwin Gooch, CBE.JP.MP - a Wymondham radical

Edwin Gooch was born in Wymondham in 1889. Arguably the most distinguished Wymondham man of the 20th century, he was the son of a blacksmith, whose business was in Fairland Street.

Then he moved to the printing trade before becoming a journalist with the Norwich Mercury. He married Ethel Banham of Wymondham who also had a distinguished public career as chair of the UDC and as a county alderman. In time Edwin became a magistrate; an active member of the Labour Party, he became the political agent for George Edwards. He supported the farm workers' strike in 1923 and served as President of the National Union of Agricultural Workers (NUAW) from 1928-61. A great champion of the working classes, he became Vice-chairman of Norfolk County Council and served on the Education Committee. As a lifelong member of the Labour Party, he served on its executive and later became the party chairman. Edwin Gooch made a big contribution to building up the Labour Party and later served as Labour MP for North Norfolk from 1945-64.

George Edwards in Wymondham 1923

Edwards, the 'farm worker's friend,' had won a bye-election as Labour candidate for South Norfolk in 1920. He was an influential supporter of the 'great strike' of 1923. Later that year, aged 73, he was successful again as Labour candidate in the general election which led to the formation of the first Labour Government. At the end of the campaign he stayed the night at Gooch's home before the count of the poll next day. After the declaration of his victory he returned to Wymondham to a great reception by a vast crowd and the New Buckenham brass band. He was escorted to the Fairland Hall which could not contain the large numbers. Speeches by Lord Kimberley and Edwin Gooch JP, were received with great enthusiasm by the audience. Later in the year, George Edwards returned to Wymondham for a party fête, at which he rejected the suggestion that the first Labour Government was in league with the Russian Bolsheviks.

George Edwards with his agent Edwin Gooch, after the victory in the by-election in 1920

The Second World War 1939-45

As Wymondham adjusted to wartime conditions, many left to join the armed forces but there was also an influx of many new faces - evacuees, allied servicemen and in 1942, American GIs.

The government's evacuation scheme moved as many children as possible, who lived in London and the large cities, to the relative safety of the countryside to escape the expected German air attacks and gas bombs. So thousands of children with name labels, gas masks and small suitcases were to find themselves far from home trying to adjust to completely new experiences.

Evacuees arrive in Wymondham - 1939

In Wymondham arrangements were planned to receive evacuees months before their actual arrival - getting camp beds and mattresses, liaising with local schools and obtaining premises for recreational centres. On 3 September the town council was informed that up to 900 children would be arriving next day. Butchers, bakers and dairies were alerted so that there would be no shortages of essential goods.

On 4 September, nearly 900 evacuees arrived after a sea journey from Gravesend to Great Yarmouth and then a bus to Wymondham. They were met by a billeting officer and others at the Fairland Hall. However, because the 'phoney war' seemed to pose no threat, most of the evacuees had returned home by January 1940. But when German bombing raids began in late 1940 two thirds of them returned to Wymondham.

The evacuees arrived at Gt Yarmouth in the Royal Daffodil

Molly, age ten years, an evacuee from Gravesend

On the boat from Gravesend, many of us were seasick and cried. I tried not to as I was older than my brother. My mum was frightened we'd be bombed before we got to Yarmouth.

When we arrived in Wymondham there were lots of grown-ups waiting for us. I wanted to go back home! They picked out the children they would have and took them away. Some brothers and sisters were separated, but me and my brother luckily went with the same people. Our new uncle and aunty had no children of their own and were very kind and welcoming to us; we had jelly and blancmange for our first tea. Uncle Bert, who worked at the local brush factory, made a swing for us in the garden. They had a lovely dog called 'Chum' and I was allowed to take him for a walk as a special treat.

We were sent to Browick School and at first we thought the locals spoke a foreign language what with their 'blast yor bores' and ' little ol gal' . But we got the hang of it and our accent was as good as theirs! We evacuees mixed and made friends with the locals; they seemed to accept us after they realised we didn't all have fleas!

A group of evacuees at the Brick Yard, Melton Road

Molly Stone (with doll), her two sisters and their adopted 'Uncle and Aunt', Mr & Mrs Myhill of Melton Road

Our new home had an oil lamp and candles for light, an open fire was used for cooking - we had rabbit stew a lot! Water came from a well in the garden. A friend of mine had never seen a cow and one day she was taken to see the milking. The cowman was squirting milk from one teat into a pail. She asked about the other three and was told they were for tea, coffee and sugar! We soon settled into life at Wymondham and really enjoyed it. Each week we went to stick a penny stamp on the big dud bomb outside the Post Office to help the town buy a Spitfire. The summers seemed endless as we played in the fields or paddled in the river. We collected mushrooms, picked apples and collected eggs; there was always something exciting to do. I began to feel a proper country girl. One day I found five bird's nests and picked hazel nuts and blackberries on the Lizard. We had nice china with matching tea cups; I never saw that before!.

One day Dad came home on leave and he brought some green bananas to Norfolk. I wondered what they were at first and why they were put in the wardrobe; then my aunt took some to her sister in Norwich but left them on the bus; Dad said he'd kept them safe for 10,000 miles and yet they managed to lose them in ten!

When the bombing raids started uncle Bert built a shelter in the garden; he was an ARP warden so I suppose it was a very good one. Next door they had a Morrison shelter in the living room - it doubled as a dining table and a shelter during air raids - the two boys used to sleep under it. We all had to carry our gas masks wherever we went. There were lots of American bases in the area and we used to look out for the sound of bombers setting off for Germany. The Yanks were very good to us kids and gave us gum, candy and sweets which was great during the rationing. My cousin had a crush on one GI but she was far too young for him!

In 1944 I saw a train arrive at the station full of wounded Yanks. A porter told me they'd been in the D Day landings and were being taken to the American hospital at Morley. Some of the soldiers looked badly injured and seeing them made me realise what war was about.

Being an evacuee was fun, a great adventure in a different world. Of course I missed home at Gravesend, and worried about my family in London. One night they lost some of their belongings in a bomb raid. It was a reminder of why I was here. My uncle and aunt were very kind to us and I will never forget being an evacuee in Wymondham during the war.

The Wymondham Regal - the silver screen lifts spirits

The Regal cinema opened in Friarscroft Lane in 1937. Its first manager was Harold Crane. The cinema soon became a popular venue in the town providing an escape from the Depression of the 1930s. With the advent of war the hardships of those years could be forgotten for a few hours as films from the 'golden age' of cinema transported people to another world of excitement, adventure and romance. Members of the armed forces stationed locally often swelled the numbers attending, as did American servicemen and other allied forces enjoying an occasional night out. News of allied successes in the war was greeted with enthusiastic cheering. Patriotic wartime slogans like 'Dig for Victory' were also shown.

After the war the Regal, now managed by Bert Caley, continued to enjoy success providing relief and escapism from the austerity of the post- war years with its ration books, fuel shortages and general economic hardship.

Decline set in during the1950s with the arrival of television and later video. Yet Les King the next manager, kept it going for another 25 years before it finally closed in 1993. However, for over half a century the Regal had played an important part in the social history of the town.

Harold Crane, first manager of the Wymondham Regal

Americans around Wymondham

The Americans began to arrive in the area in 1942. By 1943 they had major bases at Hethel, Old Buckenham, Tibenham and Deopham Green and a local HQ at Ketteringham Hall. After the D Day landings in June 1944, many wounded American soldiers arrived at Wymondham railway station. From here they were taken to the American Army Hospital at Morley, a centre of medical excellence where the use of penicillin was being trialled. By December 1944 it had admitted 2,099 casualties and a further 1,155 in 1945. After the war, the hospital eventually became a state boarding school, Wymondham College.

During the war, American and British servicemen relaxed at the Anglo-American Services Club in Town Green, now the Snooker Centre.

Mrs Pratt, Manageress of the Anglo-American Services Club

I work in the club which is used by servicemen in the area, especially Americans. Norman Brown of the Church Army is in charge; the Club was opened by Lord Walsingham and General Arnold, who later commanded the American Air Force, was also present that day.

Downstairs there is a cafeteria and upstairs is the dance hall, the most popular part of the club! Various bands play here like the 'Het Cats' from Hethel; the 'Gremlins' from Watton were really good. Sometimes we had a real treat when the 'Gable Gators' from Morley Hospital came along; my, could they play! When there is no band Norman plays dance records instead, especially Glenn Miller which everyone loves.

One of my other jobs is to chaperone the girls from the town and nearby villages when they visit the hospital at Morley. The idea is that they cheer up the patients on Sunday afternoons - well, I am not that good at chaperoning and I think the ones who were most cheered up were the girls when they saw those handsome American soldiers! We're taken to Morley by ambulance and anyway, the boys seem very pleased to see us!

Men came to this club from Hethel, Deopham, Old Buckenham and even Wendling. Sometimes it was sad to see a crew who always came together with first one and then more members missing. But no one ever said anything. People have to get on with things and enjoy whatever they can during the war. Life is precious and I'm sure the Americans who go on those bombing raids over Germany feel it as keenly as anyone. Here at the Club they can forget the horrors of war for a few hours.

One of the many American air men who were based in the Wymondham area was Daniel Hannon.

Daniel Hannon, an American pilot

I am a first pilot on a B17 attached to the 452nd Bomb Group 721 Squadron at Deopham Green. Our job is to give Hitler's Germany hell as often as we can.

The folks round here are very welcoming and good to us. They treat us real well, like family. Two local boys bring their mother's freshly baked bread to us in our hut. It's a real treat and helps to boost morale as its just like getting food from home.

Deopham Green is a tough assignment and we've just had a lucky escape. Last week while we were attacking Zietz in Germany, where there is a synthetic oil refinery, we were hit with heavy flak and when we got back to base, we discovered 43 holes in the plane's wings.

During that raid my armourer gunner Bill Houchins,was hit in the shoulder. I went down into the nose to give him first aid and morphine; we checked his oxygen level every 3 minutes. As we flew back into Deopham we sent flares up to show we had wounded on board. And as soon as we landed we were met promptly by an ambulance from the Morley hospital. We're lucky to have such a place where our boys are patched up. We were all shocked at the state of Bill and one of my crewmen thought he wouldn't fly again. But the war was not over and we were back over Germany a few days later giving those Nazis hell. And Bill? Well he's recovering well - those doctors do a grand job at Morley.

This war can be pretty grim at times, but I enjoy coming to the Anglo American Club in Wymondham. We can relax there for a few hours and try to forget the death and destruction that has become part of a our daily lives.

Brushmaking in Wymondham 1922- 1985

Its importance to the town

Though one of the oldest crafts, brushmaking is also one of the least regarded; the humble brush is usually discarded once its life is over, but brushmaking has a special place in the Wymondham story. For over a century it was the hub of the town's economy making an indelible impact on the lives of many local families. This vital part of the town's industrial heritage is preserved in the Heritage Museum. Brush production by the two main factories in the town was central to domestic and industrial life in England until the 1960s.

By 1922 brushmaking in Wymondham was about to enter its most productive period as a result of the output of two factories in the town, namely, CWS in Chapel Lane and Briton Brush, which was formed when S.D. Page & Sons amalgamated with D Matthew & Son to form Briton Brush.

The rise and rise of Briton Brush - 1922- 1965

As the industry entered its 'golden age', Briton Brush led the way. Wymondham became the centre of brushmaking in Norfolk putting the town firmly on England's industrial map. The mechanisation of production also enabled it to survive the lean years of the Depression. More brushes were made in Wymondham and Norwich than by any other firm in the country. The numbers employed steadily rose and by the mid 1920s Briton Brush products became known world-wide. 'Briton brushes sweep the world' and 'a Briton brush for every use', were two of their successful slogans.

By 1933 all manufacturing operations of the company were based in Wymondham which was the most up-to-date factory in the country. During the Second World War, Mrs Tooke worked there from 1941 making army brooms and clean sweeps for 9 shillings a week. Mr Tooke, an electrician, was paid 15 shillings a week (75p). They worked from 7.30am - 6.30pm each day and Saturday mornings as well. Briton Brush enjoyed a 'golden age' until the 1960s. During these boom years Lady's Lane became known as 'Factory Lane'.

Briton Brush - a very distinctive factory

The factory was a unique feature of the industrial and social life of the town. With its large labour force which at one time rose to over 800, it was the main employer in Wymondham until the arrival of Lotus Cars in 1966.

The range and speed of production was remarkable - 2,000 different types of brush were produced and 30,000 brushes manufactured daily.

Each day a special train left the factory with finished brushes using its own railway sidings. The railway allowed easy import of raw materials from abroad such as bristles from China, and enabled the company to meet the demands of an expanding world market efficiently.

Works entrance to Briton Brush in Lady's Lane

The business also had its own engineering workshops where new machines were designed, built, tested and developed; there was equipment for every stage of production

Briton Brush was an excellent family business whose directors took a personal interest in the welfare of workers - at one point, several generations of the same family worked there and many workers were long service employees like Mr and Mrs Reeves, who between them clocked up 100 years

Women at work in the Briton Brush factory

for the company. There were excellent amenities for workers like an active social club, canteen, sports clubs, works outings. Former employees remember trips to Clacton, Yarmouth and Samson and Hercules Dance Hall in Norwich. There were also pensioner lunches, and special buses to transport workers from outside the town to and from the factory. The company also had its own fire brigade.

In 1946 at the 200th anniversary celebrations in Norwich,there was a big welcome home for all former employees who had served in the war.

Post war difficulties and decline 1945-67

After the Second World War, the company was severely tested but the industry continued to prosper for a further 20 years or so.

An outing to the Broads (1960s), by former Briton Brush workers

Michael Marwood, Production and Technical Director, at Briton Brush

I joined the company in 1962 as Methods Engineer. In my time there, (1962-71) it employed between 500-600 people. The engineering section which built brushmaking machinery held world patents for some of its designs. The company had a long tradition of innovation. In 1936 it put in a unique system of burning its wood waste to produce electricity via a steam turbine, after which the steam was used to heat the factory. In the same year the company was the first in the brush industry to use time and motion study for costing all its products

Briton Brush was a typical family business where everyone knew everyone else. Sometimes there were several generations of the same family working there. There were football and cricket teams and annual outings.

The beginning of the end of Wymondham brushmaking

In the face of growing foreign competition Briton Brush joined the Reed Group in 1967. It merged with Chadwick Hollins and was re-named Briton Chadwick. This gave a fresh impetus to the industry as did the automatic boring machine in 1974. However, the boom was short-lived and by now only 50 workers came through the factory gates. Further decline led to a take-over by Windmill Brush Company in 1982. In 1983 the CWS factory closed and the Windmill Brush Company closed in 1985. In 1988 the 120 foot chimney stack and water tower of the CWS factory, tall symbols of the brush making industry, finally disappeared from Wymondham's skyline.

Some reasons for brushmaking's decline:

One factor was that cheap foreign competition and changes in domestic and industrial life meant a smaller brush range was needed. A demand for plastic rather than wooden articles was also damaging as was the automatic boring machine which replaced the output of ten workers on the old Gane machines.The arrival of Lotus in 1966 symbolised a new era in industrial life.

Brushmaking was to Wymondham what cotton had once been to the Lancashire towns. The spoons and spigot on the town arms, town sign and

Market Cross, together with the Brushmaker's Arms in Central Hall and names like Spooner Row and Sawyers Lane are permanent reminders of a bygone age. Though the brushmaking tradition lives on at Hamilton Acorn, descendants of Page in Attleborough, its true home is Wymondham with which the industry will always be inseparably linked.

Smaller brushmakers:

Sam Kidman - He left Page's and set up on his own as a wood-turner and brushmaker on Vimy Ridge; Sam is a reminder of the links between the ancient tradition of wood-turning by individual craftsmen and the big brush making factories of modern times. He specialised in handles and closed in 1964.

William Carter - He was a master craftsman who produced hand-made brushes in his Town Green workshop, formerly the Dove public house. He employed nine workers but was eventually forced by Board of Trade regulations to reduce this to two.

The home of William Carter on the far right

Kett's Rebellion re-enacted during the 450th anniversary celebrations in 1999

Some important events in Wymondham 1945 - 2003

1952	RC church founded as a memorial to British POWs in Far East
1963	Police station moved from the Bridewell to Fairland
1964	Kings Head hotel closed
	Wymondham /Wells railway passenger service withdrawn
1966	Wymondham Society, later Wymondham Heritage Society founded
	Lotus Cars arrived
	1st indoor bowling green at the Dell opened
1967	Fire station moved to new premises on old London Road.
1969	Town sign erected. Rail service to Dereham withdrawn
1977	Rattle Row pulled down
1983	Health Centre opened
	CWS brush factory closed
1984	Heritage Museum opened
1985	Briton Brush closed
	1st Kett Day
1989	Plaque to mark restoration of historic station by David Turner
	Market Cross restored
1990	John Ottway World Indoor bowling champion
1992	Bridewell magistrates court closed
1993	Regal Cinema closed
1995	The new one-way system opened
1996	By-pass opened
	Heritage Museum moved to restored Bridewell
	1st Wymondham Music Week
1999	'Kett 99' celebrations of 450th anniversary of Kett's Rebellion
	Mid- Norfolk Railway opened linking Wymondham with Dereham
	Swimming pool opened
2000	Ketts Park and Recreation Centre opened
	1st Farmer's Market.
	New Medical Centre opened
2001	Police station moved from the Fairland to County HQ site
2003	Wymondham Learning Centre opened

Adrian Hoare, Author and Narrator

Adrian is Chairman of the Wymondham Heritage Museum which is housed in the Bridewell, a former prison. The museum tells the story of the Bridewell, which also served as a police station and courthouse. Its many displays portray the history of Wymondham and its people, including its most famous son Robert Kett.

The museum is open from March – November

10 – 4 Mondays to Saturdays, 2 – 4 Sundays